W9-AGG-779

Polyglott

Language Guide
German

Polyglott-Verlag München

ILLUSTRATION
OF SOME IMPORTANT PHONETIC SYMBOLS

(International Phonetic Association)

[ɛ]   as *e* in pen
[ə]   as *a* in ago
[ɪ]   as *i* in bit
[ɔ]   as *o* in gone
[œ]   approx. as *i* in girl
[ø]   as *eu* in French feu
[ʒ]   as *s* in measure
[ç]   see page 5
[ŋ]   as *ng* in sing
[ʁ]   vocalized *r*
[ʃ]   as *sh* in shirt
[ː]   indicates the full length of vowels
[ʔ]   glottal stop
[']   strong stress
[ˌ]   medium stress

★

Auflage: 12. 11. 10.   9.   8. | Letzte Zahlen
Jahr: 1988 87 86 85 84 | maßgeblich

© 1964 by Polyglott GmbH.
Printed in Germany / Druckhaus Langenscheidt, Berlin
Cover: Prof. Richard Blank
ISBN 3-493-61150-1

Berlin: The Brandenburg Gate

Sprechen Sie bitte deutsch!

Speak German, please!—this request will often be made to you should you try to speak English only when travelling in Germany, Austria and Switzerland. The intention of this little phrase-book is to help you get over this language difficulty despite the lack of any previous knowledge of German. We have tried to reduce the size of this book to a minimum. By omitting all superfluous details we have made sure that you will instantly find any phrase you need. Because it is our intention that the phrases should relate to every day essentials which must be spoken, we have ignored the German terms for such objects as those parts of the body, which can be readily pointed out with an expressive hand, or any similar object.

Here are now some hints on how to make the best use of this book:

1. On the next two pages you will find a brief survey of German grammar and pronunciation. It would be advisable for you to study this before you begin your journey.

2. The book-mark inserted in the book gives a list of the essential words, sentences and phrases required for every day use. These were selected from pages 6 and 7, where they will be found

again, with some other useful phrases. 3. There are 13 chapters in this book, and each deals with a special subject occupying two pages which face each other. In general, the left-hand page will give the main questions and answers, as well as other phrases, while the right-hand page will comprise an alphabetical list of the most important words generally used, and also a boxed list of signs and notices which will most frequently recur during your travels. 4. In order to save space we have often combined sentences which would otherwise have to be repeated. These contain alternative words or phrases which we have printed in italics. As an example, page 6 contains the sentence: "Haven't you something *less expensive (better)?*"—„Haben Sie nichts *Billigeres (Besseres)?*" This stands for two sentences and can be read either as: "Haven't you something less expensive?"—„Haben Sie nichts Billigeres?" or as: "Haven't you something better?"—„Haben Sie nichts Besseres?" 5. Where asterisks are used, these are meant to indicate the questions and answers which may likely be addressed to you by the German people you meet.

And now we wish you:
Eine angenehme Reise!

3

Some Grammatical Principles

Gender and Article

There are three genders: masculine, feminine, neuter. The respective definite articles are: der [deːʁ], die [diː], das [das], the plural of all three: die [diː]; the indefinite articles: ein [aɪn], eine ['aɪnə], ein [aɪn]. There is no plural form of the indefinite article.

Declension of Nouns and Adjectives

There are 4 cases: Nominative (N), Genitive (G), Dative (D) and Accusative (A). In the vocabularies of this phrase-book the genitive/singular and the nominative/plural of nouns are given in brackets; (-) indicates that the plural is equal to the nominative/singular, and (0) indicates that the noun is not used in the plural. There are 3 different declensions of the adjective which are determined by the article.

1. With the definite article the adjective has the following endings: singular/N: der große See [deːʁ 'groːsə zeː] (the big lake), G: des ~en Sees, D: dem ~en See, A: den ~en See; plural/N: die ~en Seen, G: der ~en Seen, D: den ~en Seen, A: die ~en Seen. Sing/N: die lange Reise [diː 'laŋə 'raɪzə] (the long journey), G + D: der ~en Reise, A: die ~e Reise, pl/N: die ~en Reisen, G: der ~en Reisen, D: den ~en Reisen, A: die ~en Reisen. Sing/N: das rote Licht [das 'roːtə lɪçt] (the red light), G: des ~en Lichts, D: dem ~en Licht, A: das ~e Licht, pl/N: die ~en Lichter, G: der ~en Lichter, D: den ~en Lichtern, A: die ~en Lichter.

2. With the indefinite article the endings are: N: ein freundlicher Kellner [aɪn 'frɔyntlɪçəʁ 'kɛlnəʁ] (a friendly waiter), G: eines ~en Kellners, D: einem ~en Kellner, A: einen ~en Kellner. N: eine grüne Wiese ['aɪnə 'gryːnə 'viːzə] (a green meadow), G + D: einer ~en Wiese, A: eine ~e Wiese. N: ein gutes Hotel [aɪn 'guːtəs hoːˈtɛl] (a good hotel), G: eines ~en Hotels, D: einem ~en Hotel, A: ein ~es Hotel.

3. Without an article the adjective has the following endings: sing/N: alter Wein ['altəʁ vaɪn] (old wine), G: ~es Weines, D: ~em Wein, A: ~en Wein, pl/N: ~e Weine, G: ~er Weine, D: ~en Weinen, A: ~e Weine. Sing/N: frische Forelle ['frɪʃə foˈrɛlə] (fresh trout), G + D: ~er Forelle, A: ~e Forelle,

pl/N: ~e Forellen, G: ~er Forellen, D: ~en Forellen, A: ~e Forellen. Sing/N: stilles Dorf ['ʃtɪləs dɔʁf (quiet village), G: ~en Dorfes, D: ~en Dorf, A: ~es Dorf, pl/N: ~e Dörfer, G: ~er Dörfer, D: ~en Dörfern, A: ~ Dörfer.

Personal Pronouns

N: ich [ɪç] (I), du [duː], Sie [ziː] (you), er [eːʁ] (he), sie [ziː] (she), es [ɛs] (it), wir [viːʁ] (we), ihr [iːʁ], Sie [ziː] (you), sie [ziː] (they); G: meiner ['maɪnəʁ], deiner ['daɪnəʁ], Ihrer ['iːrəʁ], seine ['zaɪnəʁ], ihrer ['iːrəʁ], seiner / e ['zaɪnəʁ / ɛs], unser ['ʊnzəʁ], eue ['ɔyəʁ], Ihrer ['iːrəʁ], ihrer ['iːrəʁ], D: mir [miːʁ], dir [diːʁ], Ihnen ['iːnən], ihm [iːm], ihr [iːʁ], ihm [iːm], uns [ʊns] euch [ɔyç], Ihnen [iːnən], ihnen [iːnən], A: mich [mɪç], dich [dɪç], Sie [ziː], ihʁ [iːn], sie [ziː], es [ɛs], uns [ʊns], euch [ɔyç], Sie [ziː], sie [ziː].

Verbs

The verb has four singular and four plural forms. The tenses are present tense, past tense, present perfect future tense. The present perfect is formed by adding the past participle of the verb (which is normally formed by placing the prefix ge- before the stem and adding -t) to the present tense of haben (to have) or sein (to be): ich habe gesagt. The future tense is formed with the present tense of werden (to become) + the infinitive: ich werde kommen.

A) The present and past tenses of sein [zaɪn] (to be), haben ['haːbən] (to have) werden ['veːʁdən] (to become):

ich	bin	war	habe
du	bist	warst	hast
Sie	sind	waren	haben
er, sie, es	ist	war	hat
wir	sind	waren	haben
ihr	seid	wart	habt
Sie / sie	sind	waren	haben
ich	hatte	werde	wurde
du	hattest	wirst	wurdest
Sie	hatten	werden	wurden
er, sie, es	hatte	wird	wurde
wir	hatten	werden	wurden
ihr	hattet	werdet	wurdet
Sie / sie	hatten	werden	wurden

B) The endings of the present tense of the weak and strong verbs: *ich -e, du -st, er, sie, es -t, wir -en, ihr -t, Sie, sie -en.* When the infinitive stem ends in *-t* or *-d* an *e* must be inserted before a consonant ending is added (*er wartet*).

If the infinitive stem of a verb ends in *-s, -ss, -z, -tz*, only a *t* instead of *st* is added in the second person sing. (*du sitzt*). Past tense endings of the weak verbs: *ich -(e)te, du -(e)test, er -(e)te, wir -(e)ten, ihr -(e)tet, Sie, sie -(e)ten (du brauchtest, du wartetest*).

C) The most important irregular verbs: *bitten, ich bitte, bat,* past participle *gebeten* (to ask); *dürfen, ich darf, durfte, (gedurft)* (to be allowed to); *fahren, ich fahre, fuhr, gefahren* (to ride); *helfen, ich helfe, half, geholfen* (to help); *können, ich kann, konnte. (gekonnt)* can); *laufen, ich laufe, lief, gelaufen*

(to run, to go on foot); *gehen, ich gehe, ging, gegangen* (to go); *lesen, ich lese, las, gelesen* (to read); *müssen, ich muß, mußte, (gemußt)* (to be obliged to); *nehmen, ich nehme, nahm, genommen* (to take); *rufen, ich rufe, rief, gerufen* (to call); *schreiben. ich schreibe, schrieb, geschrieben* (to write); *sehen, ich sehe, sah, gesehen* (to see); *sitzen, ich sitze, saß, gesessen* (to sit); *sprechen, ich spreche, sprach, gesprochen* (to speak); *stehen, ich stehe, stand, gestanden* (to stand); *tragen, ich trage, trug, getragen* (to carry); *tun, ich tue, tat, getan* (to do); *vergessen, ich vergesse, vergaß, vergessen* (to forget); *verlieren, ich verliere, verlor, verloren* (to lose); *waschen, ich wasche, wusch, gewaschen* (to wash); *wollen, ich will, wollte, (gewollt)* (to wish); *denken, ich denke, dachte, gedacht* (to think); *wissen, ich weiß, wußte, gewußt* (to know).

... about Pronunciation

The pronunciation of words and phrases is given in the third column of each page. To begin with you will probably find it a little difficult to accustom yourself to the phonetic transcription used in this phrase-book. But if you persist you will soon realize that, having once fully grasped the symbols and the most important rules of pronunciation, your knowledge of German will be amazingly facilitated. On page 2 of this book you will find a list of all those symbols which differ from normal English letters. The list below shows the phonetic symbols in square brackets.

Vowels and Diphthongs

[a]   approximately as *u* in but
[ɑ]   as *a* in father
[ɛ]   short as *e* in get, long as *ai* in fair
[e]   as *ai* in Scotch laird
[ə]   as *a* in ago
[ɪ]   as *i* in it
[i]   as *ee* in meet
[ɔ]   as *o* in lot
[o]   as *o* in molest
[œ]   this sound resembles the *i* in girl, and should be pronounced with rounded lips
[ø]   there is no equivalent for this sound in English, it is *eu* as in French feu
[u]   as *oo* in book
[u]   as *oo* in boot

[ʏ] short ⎫ this sound may be pronounc-
[y] long   ⎬ ed by saying [i] through
       ⎭ closely rounded lips
[aɪ]   approximately as *i* in like
[aʊ]   approximately as *ou* in mouse
[ɔʏ]   approximately as *oy* in boy

Consonants

[b], [d], [f], [h], [k], [l], [m], [n], [p], [t] do not differ from the respective English consonants.
[g]   as *g* in get   [ʒ]   as *s* in measure
[j]   as *y* in year   [ʃ]   as *sh* in shop
[s]   as *ss* in kiss   [ŋ]   as *ng* in sing
[z]   as *z* in zero   [v]   as *v* in vast
[ç]   an approximation of this sound may be found by saying [ɪj] and emitting a strong current of breath
[x]   as in Scotch loch
[R]   rolled uvular *r*; English *r* as in red, cross may be substituted
[ʁ]   vocalized *r*; English *r* as in lord, garden, sure may be used
[a̯]   neutral vocalized *r*; English *er* as in father may be used
[:]   indicates the full length of the preceding vowel
[t̯]   placed over a vowel indicates that the vowel is a semi-consonant
[ʔ]   the glottal stop is the forced stop between one word or syllable and one following which begins with a vowel
[']   indicates that the syllable which follows has strong stress
[ˌ]   indicates that the syllable which follows has medium stress

5

A Few Essential Phrases

Good morning.	Guten Morgen (before noon: Guten Tag).	ˌguːtən ˈmɔʁgən (ˌguːtən ˈtaːk)
Good afternoon.	Guten Tag.	ˌguːtən ˈtaːk
Good evening.	Guten Abend.	ˌguːtən ˈaːbənt
Good night.	Gute Nacht.	ˌguːtə ˈnaxt
Good-bye.	Auf Wiedersehen.	auf ˈviːdɐˌzeː(ə)n
When *does (do)* ... open?	Wann *ist (sind)* ... geöffnet?	van ɪst (zɪnt) ... gəˈœfnət
When *does (do)* ... close?	Wann *wird (werden)* ... geschlossen?	van vɪʁt (ˌveːʁdən) ... gəˈʃlɔsən
How do I get *to* ...?	Wie komme ich *nach (zum, zur)* ...?	viː ˌkɔmə ɪç naːx (tsʊm, tsuːʁ) ...
How long will it take?	Wie lange wird es dauern?	viː ˌlaŋə vɪʁt ɛs ˈdauˌən
How far is it *to* ...?	Wie weit ist es *nach (zum, zur)* ...?	viː vait ɪst ɛs naːx (tsʊm, tsuːʁ) ...
Where can I get ...?	Wo bekomme ich ...?	voː bəˈkɔmə ɪç ...
Please let me have ...!	Geben Sie mir bitte ...!	ˌgeːbən ziː miːʁ ˌbɪtə ...
Can I get ... here?	Gibt es hier ...?	giːpt ɛs hiːʁ ...
I need ...	Ich brauche ...	ɪç ˈbʁauxə ...
I would like ...	Ich möchte ...	ɪç ˈmœçtə ...
Have you ...?	Haben Sie ...?	ˌhaːbən ziː ...
How much do you want?	Wieviel bekommen Sie?	ˌviːfiːl bəˈkɔmən ziː
How much do you charge for this?	Wieviel kostet das?	ˌviːfiːl ˈkɔstət das
How much is ...?	Wieviel kostet ...?	ˌviːfiːl ˌkɔstət ...
I like it.	Das gefällt mir.	das gəˈfɛlt miːʁ
I don't like it.	Das gefällt mir nicht.	das gəˈfɛlt miːʁ nɪçt
That is too expensive.	Das ist zu teuer.	das ɪst tsu ˈtɔɐ
Haven't you something *less expensive (better)*?	Haben Sie nicht etwas *Billigeres (Besseres)*?	ˌhaːbən ziː nɪçt ˌɛtvas ˈbiligəʁəs (ˈbɛsəʁəs)
When will it be ready?	Wann ist es fertig?	van ɪst ɛs ˈfɛʁtɪç
Can you change this?	Können Sie wechseln?	ˌkœnən ziː ˈvɛksəln
What is this called in *German (English)*?	Wie heißt das auf *deutsch (englisch)*?	viː haɪst das auf dɔʏtʃ (ˈɛŋlɪʃ)
What is the time, please?	Wie spät ist es bitte?	viː ʃpɛːt ɪst ɛs ˌbɪtə
I don't speak ...	Ich spreche kein ...	ɪç ˈʃpʁeçə kaɪn ...
I don't understand you.	Ich verstehe Sie nicht.	ɪç fɛʁˈʃteːə ziː nɪçt
Please speak more slowly.	Sprechen Sie bitte etwas langsamer!	ˌʃpʁeçən ziː ˌbɪtə ˌɛtvas ˈlaŋzaːmaˌ
How do you pronounce this word?	Wie spricht man dieses Wort aus?	viː ʃpʁɪçt man ˌdiːzəs vɔʁt ˈaus
Please write this down for me.	Schreiben Sie mir das bitte auf.	ˌʃʁaɪbən ziː miːʁ das ˌbɪtə ˈauf
Yes / no.	Ja / nein.	jaː / naɪn
Thank you.	Danke.	ˈdaŋkə
Sorry!	Verzeihung!	fɛʁˈtsaɪʊŋ
I beg your pardon!	Entschuldigen Sie!	ɛntˈʃuldigən ziː
Don't mention it!	Keine Ursache.	ˌkaɪnə ˈuːʁzaxə

Sunday / Monday......	Sonntag / Montag	'zɔntaːk / 'moːntaːk
Tuesday / Wednesday ..	Dienstag / Mittwoch ..	'diːnstaːk / 'mɪtvɔx
Thursday / Friday	Donnerstag / Freitag ..	'dɔna̯staːk / 'fʀaɪtaːk
Saturday	Sonnabend (Samstag)..	'zonaːbənt ('zamstaːk)
holiday / Easter	Feiertag / Ostern	'faɪa̯taːk / 'oːsta̯n
Whitsun / Christmas ...	Pfingsten / Weihnachten	'pfɪŋstən / 'vaɪnaxtən
January / February....	Januar / Februar	'janūaʀ / 'feːbʀūaʀ
March / April / May...	März / April / Mai....	mɛʀts / a'pʀɪl / maɪ
June / July / August ...	Juni / Juli / August....	'juːni / 'juːli / au'gʊst
September / October...	September / Oktober ..	zɛp'tɛmba̯ / ɔk'toːba̯
November / Decembe...	November / Dezember.	no'vɛmba̯ / de'tsɛmba̯
today / yesterday......	heute / gestern	'hɔʏtə / 'gɛsta̯n
tomorrow / tonight	morgen / heute abend .	'mɔʀgən / ˌhɔʏtə 'aːbənt
the day after tomorrow	übermorgen	'yːba̯mɔʀgən
this afternoon	heute nachmittag	'hɔʏtə 'naːxmɪtaːk
at noon tomorrow	morgen mittag........	ˌmɔʀgən 'mɪtaːk
tomorrow night	morgen abend	ˌmɔʀgən 'aːbənt
in the morning	vormittags	'foːʀmɪtaːks
in the afternoon	nachmittags	'naːxmɪtaːks
at *noon (midnight)*	um *Mittag* (*Mitternacht*)	ʊm 'mɪtaːk ('mɪta̯naxt)
this (next) week	*diese (nächste)* Woche.	'diːzə ('nɛːçstə) ˌvɔxə
in three *days (weeks)*..	in drei *Tagen (Wochen)*	ɪn dʀaɪ 'taːgən ('vɔxən)
at 11 a.m. / at 5 p.m....	um elf Uhr / um siebzehn Uhr	ʊm ɛlf uːʀ / ʊm 'ziːptseːn uːʀ
at a quarter *to* (past) 11 at 12 o'clock / at 12.30	um Viertel *vor (nach)* elf um zwölf Uhr / um zwölf Uhr dreißig	ʊm ˌfɪʀtəl foːʀ (naːx) ɛlf ʊm tsvœlf uːʀ / ʊm tsvœlf uːʀ 'dʀaɪsɪç
bright / dark / colourless	hell / dunkel / farblos.	hɛl / 'dʊŋkəl / 'faʀbloːs
blue / brown / green....	blau / braun / grün....	blau / bʀaun / gʀyːn
yellow / red / pink.....	gelb / rot / rosa.......	gɛlp / ʀoːt / 'ʀoːza
black / grey / white	schwarz / grau / weiß..	ʃvaʀts / gʀau / vaɪs

#	German	IPA	#	German	IPA
0	null	nʊl	21	einundzwanzig...	'aɪnʊntsvantsɪç
1	eins (ein, eine, ein)	aɪns (aɪn, 'aɪnə, aɪn)	22	zweiundzwanzig..	'tsvaɪʊntsvantsɪç
2	zwei........	tsvaɪ	30	dreißig.........	'dʀaɪsɪç
3	drei	dʀaɪ	40	vierzig	'fɪʀtsɪç
4	vier	fiːʀ	50	fünfzig..........	'fʏnftsɪç
5	fünf	fynf	60	sechzig	'zɛçtsɪç
6	sechs	zɛks	70	siebzig	'ziːptsɪç
7	sieben	'ziːbən	80	achtzig	'axtsɪç
8	acht	axt	90	neunzig	'nɔʏntsɪç
9	neun	nɔʏn	100	(ein)hundert	(aɪn)'hʊnda̯t
10	zehn	tseːn	110	(ein)hundertzehn .	(aɪn)hʊnda̯t-'tseːn
11	elf	ɛlf			
12	zwölf	tsvœlf	200	zweihundert	'tsvaɪhʊnda̯t
13	dreizehn	'dʀaɪtseːn	1000	(ein)tausend	(aɪn)'tauzənt
14	vierzehn	'fɪʀtseːn	2000	zweitausend	'tsvaɪtauzənt
15	fünfzehn	'fʏnftseːn	10.000	zehntausend	'tseːntauzənt
16	sechzehn	'zɛçtseːn	100.000	hunderttausend ..	'hʊnda̯t-ˌtauzənt
17	siebzehn	'ziːptseːn			
18	achtzehn	'axtseːn	1962	neunzehnhundert- zweiundsechzig ..	ˌnɔʏntseːn-ˌhʊnda̯t-ˌtsvaɪʊnt-ˌzɛçtsɪç
19	neunzehn	'nɔʏntseːn			
20	zwanzig	'tsvantsɪç			

half / one third	die Hälfte / ein Drittel .	diː 'hɛlftə / aɪn 'dʀɪtəl
a quarter / a tenth	ein Viertel / ein Zehntel	aɪn 'fɪʀtəl / aɪn 'tseːntəl
seconds / minutes......	Sekunden / Minuten ..	zə'kʊndən / mi'nuːtən
hours / days	Stunden / Tage	'ʃtundən / 'taːgə
weeks / months	Wochen / Monate	'vɔxən / 'moːnatə
years / centuries	Jahre / Jahrhunderte ..	'jaːʀə / jaːʀ'hʊnda̯tə
German mark(s)	Deutsche Mark	ˌdɔʏtʃə 'maʀk

!!

7

By Bus, Train, Boat, and Plane

One second class ticket single to ... please!	Einmal zweiter Klasse einfach nach ... bitte!	'ainmaːl ˌtsvaitə ˌklasə ˌainfax naːx ... ˌbitə
How long is the ticket valid?	Wie lange ist die Karte gültig?	viː 'laŋə ist diː ˌkaʁtə 'gyltiç
Which is the quickest route to ...?	Welches ist die beste Verbindung nach ...?	ˌvɛlçəs ist diː ˌbestə fɛʁˌbindʊŋ naːx ...
Is there a quicker *train (boat)*?	Gibt es einen schnelleren Zug (Dampfer)?	giːbt ɛs ˌainən 'ʃnɛləʁən tsuːk (ˌdampfə)
Where must I change?	Wo muß ich umsteigen?	voː mʊs iç 'ʊmʃtaigən
What time is the connection to ...?	Wann habe ich Anschluß nach ...?	van ˌhaːbə iç ˌanʃlʊs naːx ...
Does the train stop at ...?	Hält der Zug in ...?	hɛlt deːʁ tsuːk in ...
When should I *embark (be at the airport)*?	Wann muß ich *an Bord (auf dem Flugplatz)* sein?	van mʊs iç an 'bɔʁt (auf deːm 'fluːkplats) zain
From which platform does the train to ... leave?	Auf welchem Bahnsteig fährt der Zug nach ... ab?	auf 'vɛlçəm ˌbaːnʃtaik feːʁt deːʁ tsuːk naːx ... 'ap
Which platform for the train to ...?	Wo fährt der Zug nach ... ab?	voː fɛːʁt deːʁ tzuːx naːx ... 'ap
Where does the train arrive from ...?	Wo kommt der Zug aus ... an?	voː kɔmt deːʁ tsuːk aʊs ... 'an
When is the train for ... due?	Wann läuft der Zug nach ... ein?	van lɔyft deːʁ tsuːk naːx ... 'ain
How long *do we (do I)* stop here?	Wie lange *haben wir (habe ich)* Aufenthalt?	viː ˌlaŋə ˌhaːbən viːʁ (ˌhaːbə iç) 'aufənthalt
Where does this train go to?	Wohin fährt dieser Zug?	voːhin 'fɛːʁt ˌdiːzə tsuːk
Where is this boat from?	Woher kommt dieser Dampfer?	voːheːʁ 'kɔmt ˌdiːzə ˌdampfə
When do we arrive at ...?	Wann kommen wir in ... an?	van ˌkɔmən viːʁ in ... 'an
Is the train late?	Hat der Zug Verspätung?	hat deːʁ tsuːk fɛʁ'ʃpɛːtʊŋ
Has this train *a dining-car, (a sleeping-car, a through-coach to ...)*?	Hat der Zug *einen Speisewagen (einen Schlafwagen, einen Kurswagen nach ...)*?	hat deːʁ tsuːk ˌainən 'ʃpaizəvaːgən, (ˌainən 'ʃlaːfvaːgən, ˌainən 'kuʁsvaːgən naːx ...)
I should like to register my case(s) as luggage.	Ich möchte *meinen (meine)* Koffer als Reisegepäck aufgeben.	iç ˌmœçtə ˌmainən (ˌmainə) ˌkɔfə als 'ʁaizəˌpɛk ˌaufgeːbən
Fetch me my luggage, please!	Holen Sie bitte mein Gepäck!	ˌhoːlən ziː ˌbitə main gə'pɛk
Take my luggage *to the train to ... (on platform ..., to the left-luggage office)*, please!	Bringen Sie mein Gepäck *zum Zug nach ... (auf Bahnsteig ..., zur Aufbewahrung)*, bitte!	ˌbriŋən ziː main gə'pɛk tsum tsuːk naːx ... (auf ˌbaːnʃtaik ..., tsuʁ 'aufbəˌvaːʁʊŋ), ˌbitə
Excuse me, is this seat taken?	Verzeihung, ist dieser Platz besetzt?	fɛʁ'tsaiʊŋ ist ˌdiːzə plats bə'zetst
This is my seat.	Dies ist mein Platz.	diːs ist 'main plats
Have a pleasant journey!	Angenehme Reise!	ˌangəneːmə 'ʁaizə

8

aeroplane	das Flugzeug (-s; -e) ..	'fluːktsɔʏk
airport	der Flughafen (-s; ⸚) ..	'fluːkhaːfən
arrival	die Ankunft (-; ⸚e) ...	'ankʊnft
boat	der Dampfer (-s; -) ...	'dampfɑ
booking-office	die Fahrkartenausgabe (-; -n)	'faːʁkaʁtənˌaʊsgaːbə
bus	der Autobus (-; -se) ..	'aʊtobʊs
cabin	die Kabine (-; -n)....	ka'biːnə
children's ticket	die Kinderfahrkarte (-; -n)	'kɪndɑˌfɑːʁkaʁtə
compartment	das Abteil (-s; -e)	ap'taɪl
connection	der Anschluß (-sses; ⸚sse)	'anʃlʊs
departure	die Abfahrt (-; -en) ..	'apfɑːʁt
dining-car	der Speisewagen (-s; -)	'ʃpaɪzəvaːgən
double berth	das Doppelbettabteil (-s; -e)	'dɔpəlbɛt'apˌtaɪl
express through train ..	der Fernschnellzug (-s; ⸚e)	'fɛʁnʃnɛltsuːk
express train	der Schnellzug (-s; ⸚e)	'ʃnɛltsuːk
excess fare	der Zuschlag (-s; ⸚e)..	'tsuːʃlɑːk
guard	der Schaffner (-s; -) ..	'ʃafnɑ
left-luggage office	die Gepäckaufbewahrung (-; -en)	gə'pɛk'aʊfbəˌvaːRʊŋ
local train	der Personenzug (-s; ⸚e)	pɛʁ'zoːnəntsuːk
luggage	das Gepäck (-s; -)....	gə'pɛk
luggage office	die Gepäckabfertigung (-; -en)	gə'pɛk'apfɛʁtigʊŋ
luggage-ticket	der Gepäckschein (-s; -e)	gə'pɛkʃaɪn
motor-boat	das Motorboot (-s; -e)	'moːtoːʁboːt
platform	der Bahnsteig (-s; -e).	'baːnʃtaɪk
platform-ticket	die Bahnsteigkarte (-; -n)	'baːnʃtaɪkkaʁtə
porter	der Gepäckträger (-s;-)	gə'pɛktʁɛːgɑ
railway-guide	das Kursbuch (-es; ⸚er)	'kuʁsbuːx
return-ticket	die Rückfahrkarte (-; -n)	'ʁʏkfɑːʁkaʁtə
single berth	das Einbettabteil (-s; -e)	'aɪnbɛt'apˌtaɪl
sleeper-reservation	die Bettkarte (-; -n) ..	'bɛtkaʁtə
sleeping-car	der Schlafwagen (-s; -)	'ʃlaːfvaːgən
station	der Bahnhof (-s; ⸚e)..	'baːnhoːf
ticket	die Fahrkarte (-; -n)..	'fɑːʁkaʁtə
ticket for a reserved seat	die Platzkarte (-; -n)..	'platskaʁtə
time-table	der Fahrplan (-s; ⸚e)..	'fɑːʁplaːn
tourist coach	der Reisebus (-; -se)..	'ʁaɪzəbʊs
tourist office	das Reisebüro (-s; -s).	'ʁaɪzəbyˌʁoː
train	der Zug (-es; ⸚e)	tsuːk

AUSGANG	Exit	NICHTRAUCHER	Non-smoker
BESETZT	Engaged	NOTAUSGANG	Emergency exit
DAMEN	Ladies	NOTBREMSE	Emergency brake
EINGANG	Entrance		
FAHRKARTEN	Tickets	RAUCHER	Smoker
FREI	Free	TOILETTEN	Public conveniences
HANDGEPÄCK	Hand-luggage		
HERREN	Gentlemen	WARTESAAL	Waiting-room

9

Travelling on Foreign Roads

Which is the *shortest (best)* way to ...?	Welches ist der *kürzeste (beste)* Weg nach ...?	ˌvɛlçəs ɪst deːʁ ˌkyʁtsəstə (ˌbɛstə) veːk naːx ...
How many *kilometres (minutes)* is it to ...? Does this road lead *to* ...?	Wie viele *Kilometer (Minuten)* sind es bis ...? Führt diese Straße *nach (zum, zur)* ...?	viː ˈfiːlə kiloˈmeːtɐ (miˈnuːtən) zɪnt ɛs bɪs ... fyːʁt ˌdiːzə ˌʃtʁɑːsə naːx (tsʊm, tsuʁ) ...?
How do I get to *the castle (the cathedral, the ... church, the market-place, the town-hall, the palace)*?	Wie komme ich *zur Burg (zum Dom, zur ... Kirche, zum Marktplatz, zum Rathaus, zum Schloß)*?	viː ˈkɔmə ɪç tsuʁ ˈbuʁk (tsʊm ˈdoːm, tsuʁ ... ˌkɪʁçə, tsʊm ˈmaʁktplats, tsʊm ˈʁɑːthaʊs, tsʊm ˈʃlɔs)
Where is *the old town, (the British, American, Irish, Indian consulate, the picture-gallery, the museum, the park)*?	Wo ist *die Altstadt, (das Britische, Amerikanische, Irische, Indische Konsulat, die Gemäldegalerie, das Museum, der Park)*?	voː ɪst diː ˈaltʃtat (das ˈbʁɪtɪʃə, ameʁiˈkɑːnɪʃə, ˈiːʁɪʃə, ˈɪndɪʃə konzuˈlɑːt, diː ɡəˈmɛːldəɡaləˈʁiː, das muˈzeːʊm, deːʁ paʁk)
Where is *the* nearest ...?	Wo ist *der (die, das)* nächste ...?	voː ɪst deːʁ (diː, das) ˌnɛːçstə ...
What are the objects of interest here?	Welche Sehenswürdigkeiten gibt es hier?	ˌvɛlçə ˌzeːənsvyʁdɪçkaɪtən ˈɡiːpt ɛs hiːʁ
When is the next conducted tour?	Wann ist die nächste Führung?	van ɪst diː ˌnɛːçstə ˈfyːʁʊŋ
Could you kindly show me this on the map?	Zeigen Sie mir das bitte auf der Karte!	ˈtsaɪɡən ziː miːʁ das ˌbɪtə aʊf deːʁ ˈkaʁtə
How far is it to walk *to* ...?	Wie weit ist es zu Fuß *nach (zum, zur)* ...?	viː vaɪt ɪst ɛs tsu fuːs naːx (tsʊm, tsuːʁ) ...
Is there *a bus (a boat, a tram)* to ...?	Fährt *ein Bus (ein Dampfer, eine Straßenbahn)* nach ...?	fɛːʁt aɪn bʊs (aɪn ˈdampfɐ, ˌaɪnə ˈʃtʁɑːsənbaːn) naːx ...
One (three) single to ..., please!	Bitte *einen (drei)* Fahrschein(e) nach ...!	ˌbɪtə ˈaɪnən (dʁaɪ) ˈfɑːʁʃaɪn(ə) naːx ...
When does the next tram go to ...?	Wann fährt die nächste Straßenbahn nach ...?	van fɛːʁt diː ˌnɛːçstə ˈʃtʁɑːsənbaːn naːx ...
How much is it to ...?	Wieviel kostet die Fahrt nach ...?	ˈviːviːl ˌkɔstət diː faːʁt naːx ...
Will you kindly tell me when I must *get out (change)*?	Sagen Sie mir bitte, wenn ich *aussteigen (umsteigen)* muß!	ˌzɑːɡən ziː miːʁ ˌbɪtə vɛn ɪç ˈaʊsʃtaɪɡən (ˈumʃtaɪɡən) mʊs
What is this ... called?	Wie heißt dies ...?	viː haɪst diːs ...
Please fill her up on ...	Bitte tanken Sie voll mit ...!	ˌbɪtə ˈtaŋkən ziː fɔl mɪt ...
Give me 10 litres.	Ich möchte 10 Liter.	ɪç ˌmœçtə tseːn ˈliːtɐ
Can one take photographs here?	Darf man hier fotografieren?	daʁf man hiːʁ fotoɡʁaˈfiːʁən
Is it allowed to camp here?	Darf man hier zelten?	daʁf man hiːʁ ˈtsɛltən
*You are on the *right (wrong)* road.	Sie sind auf dem *richtigen (falschen)* Weg.	ziː zɪnt aʊf deːm ˈʁɪçtiɡən (ˈfalʃən) veːk
*You must *drive (keep)* straight on.	Sie müssen geradeaus *fahren (gehen)*.	ziː ˌmysən ɡəˌʁɑːdəˈaʊs ˌfaːʁən (ˌgeːən)
*You must *keep* to the *left (right)*.	Sie müssen sich *links (rechts)* halten.	ziː ˌmysən zɪç ˈlɪŋks (ˈʁɛçts) ˌhaltən
*You must not *drive (walk)* here.	Hier dürfen Sie nicht *fahren (gehen)*.	hiːʁ ˌdyʁfən ziː nɪçt ˈfaːʁən (ˈgeːən)

10

autocycle	das Moped *(-s; -s)* ..	'moːpɛt
bicycle	das Fahrrad *(-es; ̈er)*.	'faːʀɑːt
bridge	die Brücke *(-; -n)* ...	'bʀʏkə
building	das Gebäude *(-s; -)*...	gə'bɔʏdə
car	das Auto *(-s; -s)*	'aʊto
car documents	die Autopapiere *pl.*...	'aʊtopaˌpiːʀə
car park	der Parkplatz *(-es; ̈e)*	'paʀkplats
coach	der Autobus *(-ses; -se)*	'aʊtobʊs
crossing	die Kreuzung *(-; -en)*.	'kʀɔʏtsʊŋ
detour	der Umweg *(-s; -e)*...	'ʊmveːk
Diesel oil	das Dieselöl *(-s; -e)*...	'diːzəlˀøːl
district	die Umgebung *(-; -en)*	ʊm'geːbʊŋ
driving licence	der Führerschein *(-s; -e)*	'fyːʀɐˌʃaɪn
footpath	der Fußweg *(-es; -e)*..	'fuːsveːk
funicular railway	die Drahtseilbahn *(-; -en)*..........	'dʀɑːtzaɪlbɑːn
moped	das Moped *(-s; -s)*....	'moːpɛt
motor-cycle	das Motorrad *(es; ̈er)*	'moːtoʀʀɑːt
motor oil	das Motorenöl *(-s; -e)*	mo'toːʀənˀøːl
motor scooter	der Motorroller *(-s; -)*	'moːtoʀʀolɐ
motorway	die Autobahn *(-; -en)*	'aʊtobɑːn
petrol	das Benzin *(-s; -)*.....	bɛn'tsiːn
petrol station	die Tankstelle *(-; -n)*..	'taŋkʃtɛlə
place	der Ort *(-es; -e)*......	ɔʀt
right of way	die Vorfahrt *(-; -)*....	'foːʀfaːʀt
road map	die Straßenkarte *(-;-n)*	'ʃtʀɑːsənkaʀtə
side-street	die Seitenstraße *(-; -n)*	'zaɪtənʃtʀɑːsə
sight-seeing tour	die Stadtrundfahrt *(-; -en)*..........	'ʃtatʀʊntfaːʀt
stop	die Haltestelle *(-; -n)* .	'haltəʃtɛlə
street	die Straße *(-; -n)*.....	'ʃtʀɑːsə
street number	die Hausnummer *(-; -n)*	'haʊsnʊmɐ
suburb	der Vorort *(-es; -e)* ..	'foːʀˀɔʀt
taxi	das Taxi *(-s; -s)*	'taksiː
tourist office	das Reisebüro *(-s; -s)*.	'ʀaɪzəbyˌʀoː
town	die Stadt *(-; ̈e)*......	ʃtat
town plan	der Stadtplan *(-s; ̈e)*.	'ʃtatplɑːn
underground	die U-Bahn *(-; -en)*...	'uːbɑːn
village	das Dorf *(-es; ̈er)*....	dɔʀf

ACHTUNG	Caution	NACH LINKS	Turn left
AUSFAHRT	Way out	NACH RECHTS	Turn right
EINBAHNSTRASSE		NATURSCHUTZGEBIET	
	One-way street		Nature reserve
EINFAHRT	Way in	PARKPLATZ	Car park
GERADEAUS	Straight on	PARKVERBOT	No waiting
GESCHLOSSEN	Closed	REPARATURWERKSTATT	
GESPERRT	Closed to traffic		Repair shop
HALT	Stop	SACKGASSE	Blind alley
HALTESTELLE	Stop	SCHLECHTE	WEGSTRECKE
HÖCHSTGESCHWINDIG-			Bad road
KEIT	Speed limit	STEINSCHLAG	Rock-fall
KEIN ZUGANG	No entry	TANKSTELLE	Petrol station
LANGSAM FAHREN		TRINKWASSER	Drinking-water
	Drive slowly	UMLEITUNG	Diversion
LEBENSGEFAHR		VERBOTEN	Prohibited
	Danger	VORSICHT	Caution
NICHT ÜBERHOLEN			
	No overtaking		

In Case Your Car Breaks Down

I have a puncture.	Ich habe eine Reifen-panne.	iç ˌhɑːbə ˌainə ˈraifən-panə
I have had an accident.	Ich habe einen Unfall gehabt.	iç ˌhɑːbə ˌainən ˈunfal gəˌhɑːpt
I had a fall.	Ich bin gestürzt.	iç bin gəˈʃtyrtst
My *car (motor-cycle, bicycle)* is ...	Mein *Wagen (Motorrad, Fahrrad)* steht ...	main ˈvɑːgən (ˈmoːtoʁ-rɑːt, ˈfaːʁrɑːt) ʃteːt ...
Could you give me a lift?	Würden Sie mich ein Stück mitnehmen?	ˌvyʁdən ziː miç ain ʃtyk ˈmitneːmən
Please give me a hand!	Bitte helfen Sie mir!	ˌbitə ˈhɛlfən ziː miːʁ
Please inform ...!	Verständigen Sie ...!	fɛʁˈʃtɛndigən ziː ...
Can you give me a tow?	Können Sie meinen Wagen abschleppen?	ˌkœnən ziː ˌmainən ˈvɑː-gən ˈapʃlɛpən
The engine *stalls (won't start)*.	Der Motor *setzt aus (springt nicht an)*.	deːʁ ˈmoːtoʁ zɛtst aus (ʃpriŋt niçt an)
... is defective.	... ist defekt.	... ist deˈfɛkt
... should be replaced.	... muß *(müssen)* er-neuert werden.	... mus (ˌmysən) ɛʁˈnɔyɑ̯t ˌveːʁdən
Please	**Bitte**	ˈbitə
– charge the battery.	– laden Sie die Batterie auf.	– ˌlɑːdən ziː diː batəˈriː auf
– adjust the brakes.	– stellen Sie die Brem-sen nach.	– ˌʃtɛlən ziː diː ˈbrɛmzən nɑːx
– check the brakes.	– prüfen Sie die Brem-sen.	– ˌpryːfən ziː diː ˈbrɛm-zən
– *mend (lubricate)* the chain.	– *flicken (ölen)* Sie die Kette.	– ˌflikən (ˌøːlən) ziː diː ˈketə
– check the water.	– füllen Sie das Kühl-wasser nach.	– ˌfylən ziː das ˈkyːl-vasə̯ nɑːx
– check the clutch.	– sehen Sie die Kupp-lung nach.	– ˌzeːən ziː diː ˈkupluŋ nɑːx
– adjust the steering.	– sehen Sie die Lenkung nach.	– ˌzeːən ziː diː ˈlɛŋkuŋ nɑːx
– check the oil level.	– prüfen Sie den Öl-stand.	– ˌpryːfən ziː deːn ˈøːl-ʃtant
– make an oil-change.	– machen Sie einen Öl-wechsel.	– ˌmaxən ziː ˌainən ˈøːl-vɛksəl
– blow up the tyres.	– pumpen Sie die Reifen auf.	– ˌpumpən ziː diː ˈraifən auf
– mend the tyre.	– flicken Sie den Reifen.	– ˌflikən ziː deːn ˈraifən
– check the tyre pressure.	– prüfen Sie den Reifen-druck.	– ˌpryːfən ziː deːn ˈrai-fəndruk
– wipe the wind screen.	– putzen Sie die Scheiben.	– ˌputsən ziː diː ˈʃaibən
– change the fuses.	– wechseln Sie die Siche-rungen aus.	– ˌvɛksəln ziː diː ˈziçə-ruŋən aus
– check the valves.	– pusten Sie die Ventile durch.	– ˌpuːstən ziː diː vɛn-ˈtiːlə durç
– adjust the carburettor.	– stellen Sie den Ver-gaser ein.	– ˌʃtɛlən ziː deːn fɛʁ-ˈgɑːzə̯ ain
– grease the car.	– schmieren Sie den Wagen ab.	– ˌʃmiːrən ziː deːn ˈvɑː-gən ap
– wash the car.	– waschen Sie den Wa-gen.	– ˈvaʃən ziː deːn ˌvɑːgən
– check the trafficators.	– überprüfen Sie die Winker.	– yːbə̯ˌpryːfən ziː diː ˈviŋkə̯
– *change (clean)* the sparking plugs.	– *erneuern (reinigen)* Sie die Zündkerzen.	– ɛʁˌnɔyɑ̯n (ˈrainigən) ziː diː ˈtsyntkɛʁtsən
– check the ignition.	– stellen Sie die Zün-dung nach.	– ˌʃtɛlən ziː diː ˈtsynduŋ nɑːx

accelerator	das Gaspedal *(-s; -e)*	ˈgɑːspeˌdɑːl
axle	die Achse *(-; -n)*	ˈaksə
backfire	die Fehlzündung *(-; -en)*	ˈfeːltsʏndʊŋ
ball bearings	das Kugellager *(-s; -)*	ˈkuːgəlɑːgɐ
battery	die Batterie *(-; -n)*	batəˈʀiː
brake	die Bremse *(-; -n)*	ˈbʀɛmzə
brake fluid	die Bremsflüssigkeit *(-; -en)*	ˈbʀɛmsflʏsɪçkaɪt
brake lining	der Bremsbelag *(-s; ⁻e)*	ˈbʀɛmsbəˌlaːk
cable	das Kabel *(-s; -)*	ˈkaːbəl
can	der Kanister *(-s; -)*	kaˈnɪstɐ
carburettor	der Vergaser *(-s; -)*	fɛʀˈgaːzɐ
clutch	die Kupplung *(-; -en)*	ˈkʊplʊŋ
clutch lining	der Kupplungsbelag *(-es; ⁻e)*	ˈkʊplʊŋsbəˌlaːk
crank-shaft	die Kurbelwelle *(-; -n)*	ˈkʊʀbəlvɛlə
cylinder	der Zylinder *(-s; -)*	tsiˈlɪndɐ
dynamo	die Lichtmaschine *(-; -n)*	ˈlɪçtmaˌʃiːnə
engine	der Motor *(-s; -en)*	ˈmoːtoʀ
exhaust pipe	der Auspuff *(-s; -e)*	ˈauspuf
gear-change	die Gangschaltung *(-; -en)*	ˈgaŋʃaltʊŋ
gearing	das Getriebe *(-s; -)*	gəˈtʀiːbə
headlight	der Scheinwerfer *(-s;-)*	ˈʃaɪnvɛʀfɐ
horn	die Hupe *(-; -n)*	ˈhuːpə
insulation	die Isolierung *(-; -en)*	izoˈliːʀʊŋ
jack	der Wagenheber *(-s; -)*	ˈvaːgənheːbɐ
lights	die Lampen *pl.*	ˈlampən
oil	das Öl *(-s; -e)*	øːl
pedal	das Pedal *(-s; -e)*	peˈdaːl
petrol pipe	die Benzinzufuhr *(-; -en)*	bɛnˈtsiːntsufuːʀ
petrol tank	der Benzintank *(-s; -s)*	bɛnˈtsiːntaŋk
piston ring	der Kolbenring *(-es; -e)*	ˈkɔlbənʀɪŋ
radiator	der Kühler *(-s;-)*	ˈkyːlɐ
repair	die Reparatur *(-; -en)*	ʀepaʀaˈtuːʀ
reserve tank	der Reservetank *(-s; -s)*	ʀeˈzɛʀvətaŋk
reverse gear	der Rückwärtsgang *(-es; ⁻e)*	ˈʀʏkvɛʀtsgaŋ
screw	die Schraube *(-; -n)*	ˈʃʀaubə
sealing	die Dichtung *(-; -en)*	ˈdɪçtʊŋ
seat-belt	der Sicherheitsgurt *(-es; -e)*	ˈzɪçɐhaɪtsgʊʀt
shock-absorber	der Stoßdämpfer *(-s; -)*	ˈʃtoːsdɛmpfɐ
spare part	der Ersatzteil *(-s; -e)*	ɛʀˈzatstaɪl
spare wheel	das Ersatzrad *(-es; ⁻er)*	ɛʀˈzatsʀaːt
speedometer	der Tachometer *(-s; -)*	taxoˈmeːtɐ
springing	die Federung *(-; -en)*	ˈfeːdəʀʊŋ
starter	der Anlasser *(-s; -)*	ˈanlasɐ
steering	die Lenkung *(-; -0)*	ˈlɛŋkʊŋ
steering wheel	das Steuerrad *(-es; ⁻er)*	ˈʃtɔyɐʀaːt
tool kit	das Werkzeug *(-s; -e)*	ˈvɛʀktsɔyk
traffic indicator	der Winker *(-s; -)*	ˈvɪŋkɐ
tyre	der Reifen *(-s; -)*	ˈʀaɪfən
tyre pump	die Luftpumpe *(-; -n)*	ˈluftpumpə
valve	das Ventil *(-s; -e)*	vɛnˈtiːl
wind-screen wiper	der Scheibenwischer *(-s; -)*	ˈʃaɪbənvɪʃɐ

Looking for a Room

Can you recommend a good (reasonably expensive) hotel?	Können Sie ein gutes (nicht zu teures) Hotel empfehlen?	ˌkœnən ziː aɪn ˌguːtəs (nɪçt tsu ˌtɔʏʀəs) hoˈtɛl emˌpfeːlən
Can I have a (moderately priced) room?	Haben Sie ein (nicht zu teures) Zimmer frei?	ˌhaːbən ziː aɪn (nɪçt tsu ˌtɔʏʀəs) ˈtsɪma̯ fʀaɪ
*There is only one room left at ...	Wir haben nur noch ein Zimmer zu ...	viːʀ ˌhaːbən nuːʀ nɔx aɪn ˈtsɪma̯ tsuː ...
*I am afraid all rooms are booked.	Wir haben (leider) nichts frei.	viːʀ ˌhaːbən ˈlaɪda̯ nɪçts fʀaɪ
*Perhaps there will be a room tomorrow.	Vielleicht wird morgen etwas frei.	fiːlaɪçt vɪʀt ˈmɔʀɡən ˌɛtvas fʀaɪ
Is it of any use to look in again later on?	Hat es Zweck, daß ich später wiederkomme?	hat ɛs tsvɛk das ɪç ˈʃpɛːta̯ ˌviːda̯kɔmə
How much do you charge for room and full board (bed and breakfast)?	Wieviel kostet ein Zimmer mit Vollpension (mit Frühstück)?	ˌviːfiːl ˌkɔstət aɪn ˌtsɪma̯ mɪt ˈfɔlpaŋˌzĭoːn (mɪt ˈfʀyːʃtyk)
Is breakfast included?	Mit Frühstück?	mɪt ˈfʀyːʃtyk
Without breakfast?	Ohne Frühstück?	ˈoːnə ˈfʀyːʃtyk
*Including (without) service?	Mit (ohne) Bedienung?	mɪt (ˈoːnə) bəˌdiːnuŋ
Is there a private bath (balcony) with the room?	Hat das Zimmer ein Bad (einen Balkon)?	hat das ˈtsɪma̯ aɪn baːt (ˌaɪnən balˈkɔŋ)
Has the room running (warm) water?	Hat das Zimmer fließendes (warmes) Wasser?	hat das ˌtsɪma̯ ˈfliːsəndəs (ˈvaʀməs) ˈvasa̯
Could I have a look at the room?	Kann ich das Zimmer sehen?	kan ɪç das ˌtsɪma̯ ˈzeːən
I should like to see another (a cheaper) room.	Ich möchte ein anderes (billigeres) Zimmer sehen.	ɪç ˌmœçtə aɪn ˈandəʀəs (ˈbɪligəʀəs) ˌtsɪma̯ ˌzeːən
I'll stay for one night only (... days, ... weeks).	Ich bleibe nur eine Nacht (... Tage, ... Wochen).	ɪç ˌblaɪbə nuːʀ ˈaɪnə naxt (... ˈtaːgə, ... ˈvɔxən)
Is there a parking place (a garage) nearby?	Ist ein Parkplatz (eine Garage) in der Nähe?	ɪst aɪn ˈpaʀkplats (ˌaɪnə gaˈʀaːʒə) ɪn deːʀ ˈnɛːə
My luggage is in the car (at the station).	Mein Gepäck ist im Wagen (am Bahnhof).	maɪn gəˌpɛk ɪst ɪm ˈvaːgən (am ˈbaːnhoːf)
Could I have breakfast in my room?	Kann ich auf dem Zimmer frühstücken?	kan ɪç aʊf deːm ˈtsɪma̯ ˈfʀyːʃtykən
What time do you serve breakfast?	Wann gibt es Frühstück?	van giːpt ɛs ˈfʀyːʃtyk
What is the voltage here?	Wie ist hier die Stromspannung?	viː ɪst hiːʀ diː ˈʃtʀoːmʃpanuŋ
Are there any letters for me?	Ist Post für mich da?	ɪst pɔst fyːʀ mɪç daː
I'll be back in about an hour (two hours).	Ich bin in einer Stunde (zwei Stunden) zurück.	ɪç bɪn ɪn ˈaɪna̯ ˈʃtundə (tsvaɪ ˈʃtundən) tsuˈʀʏk
I'll leave tonight (tomorrow morning).	Ich reise heute abend (morgen früh) ab.	ɪç ˌʀaɪzə ˌhɔʏtə ˈaːbənt (ˌmɔʀgən ˈfʀyː) ˈap
I should like to be called at ... o'clock.	Ich möchte um ... Uhr geweckt werden.	ɪç ˌmœçtə ʊm ... uːʀ gəˈvɛkt ˌveːʀdən
Please forward my letters to this address: ...	Schicken Sie bitte meine Post an diese Adresse nach: ...	ˌʃɪkən ziː ˌbɪtə ˌmaɪnə pɔst an ˈdiːzə aˈdʀɛsə naːx ...

14

balcony	der Balkon (-s; -s)	bal'kɔŋ
bath	das Bad (-es; ʺer)	baːt
bill	die Rechnung (-; -en)	'ʀɛçnuŋ
boarding house	die Pension (-; -en)	paŋ'zĭoːn
breakfast room	das Frühstückszimmer (-s; -)	'fʀyːʃtʏks͵tsɪmaʼ
chamber-maid	das Zimmermädchen (-s; -)	'tsɪmaʼmɛːtçən
clothes-brush	die Kleiderbürste (-; -n)	'klaɪdaʼbʏʀstə
clothes-hanger	der Kleiderbügel (-s;-)	'klaɪdaʼbyːgəl
door-keeper	der Portier (-s; -s)	pɔʀ'tĭeː
dining-room	der Speisesaal (-s; ʺe)	'ʃpaɪzəzaːl
director	der Direktor (-s; -en)	di'ʀɛktoʀ
double room	das Doppelzimmer (-s; -)	'dɔpəltsɪmaʼ
down-payment	die Anzahlung (-; -en)	'antsaːluŋ
floor	das Stockwerk (-s; -e)	'ʃtɔkvɛʀk
garage	die Garage (-; -n)	ga'ʀɑːʒə
heating	die Heizung (-; -en)	'haɪtsuŋ
hotel	das Hotel (-s; -s)	ho'tɛl
inn	der Gasthof (-s; ʺe)	'gasthoːf
key	der Schlüssel (-s; -)	'ʃlʏsəl
latch-key	der Hausschlüssel (-s; -)	'hausʃlʏsəl
lavatory	die Toilette (-; -n)	tŏa'letə
lift	der Fahrstuhl (-s; ʺe)	'faːʀʃtuːl
luggage	das Gepäck (-s; 0)	gə'pɛk
manager	der Geschäftsführer (-s; -)	gə'ʃɛftsfyːʀaʼ
parking place	der Parkplatz (-es; ʺe)	'paʀkplats
piece of soap	ein Stück Seife	aɪn ʃtʏk 'zaɪfə
pillow	das Kissen (-s; -)	'kɪsən
porter	der Gepäckträger (-s; -)	gə'pɛktʀɛgaʼ
registration	die Anmeldung (-; -en)	'anmɛlduŋ
room	das Zimmer (-s; -)	'tsɪmaʼ
service	die Bedienung (-; -en) der Dienst (-es; -e)	bə'diːnuŋ / diːnst
single bed	das Einzelbett (-s; -en)	'aɪntsəlbɛt
single room	das Einzelzimmer (-s; -)	'aɪntsəltsɪmaʼ
sleeping-bag	der Schlafsack (-s; ʺe)	'ʃlaːfzak
tip	das Trinkgeld (-es; -er)	'tʀɪŋk(g)ɛlt
towel	das Handtuch (-s; ʺer)	'hantuːx
twin-bed	das Doppelbett (-s; -en)	'dɔpəlbɛt
waiter	der Kellner (-s; -) / Ober (-s; -)	'kɛlnaʼ / 'oːbaʼ
warden	der Herbergsvater (-s; ʺ)	'hɛʀbɛʀksfaːtaʼ
wash-basin	das Waschbecken (-s; -)	'vaʃbɛkən
Youth Hostel	die Jugendherberge (-; -n)	'juːgənt͵hɛʀbɛʀgə

BAD	bath	KALT	cold
DAMEN	ladies	TOILETTE	lavatory
HERREN	gentlemen	WARM	warm
HOTEL BESETZT		ZIMMER FREI	room free
	no vacancies		

In Restaurants and Cafés

Can you recommend a *good (cheap)* restaurant? | Können Sie ein *gutes (billiges)* Restaurant empfehlen? | ˌkœnən ziː aɪn ˈguːtəs (ˈbɪliɡəs) ʀɛstoˈʀaŋ ɛmˌpfeːlən

Where can one get a good (and inexpensive) meal? | Wo kann man gut (und nicht zu teuer) essen? | voː kan man guːt (ʊnt nɪçt tsu ˈtɔʏʌ) ˈɛsən

I need a table for ... persons. | Ich brauche einen Tisch für ... Personen. | ɪç ˌbʀauxə ˌaɪnən tɪʃ fyːʀ ... pɛʀˈzoːnən

Has this *seat (table)* been taken? | Ist dieser *Platz (Tisch)* besetzt? | ɪst ˌdiːzʌ plats (tɪʃ) bəˈzɛtst

Waiter (waitress), the menu, please! | *Herr Ober (Fräulein)*, die Speisekarte bitte! | hɛʀ ˈoːbʌ (ˈfʀɔʏlaɪn) diː ˈʃpaɪzəkaʀtə ˌbɪtə

Can you recommend a speciality for which this place is famous? | Können Sie mir eine Spezialität Ihres Hauses empfehlen? | ˌkœnən ziː miːʀ ˌaɪnə ʃpeːtsiɑliˈtɛt ˌiːʀəs ˌhauzəs ɛmˈpfeːlən

Please bring me ...! | Bringen Sie mir bitte...! | ˌbʀɪŋən ziː miːʀ ˌbɪtə ...

I shall take the set meal for ... | Ich möchte das Gedeck zu ... | ɪç ˌmœçtə das ɡəˌdɛk tsu ...

A la carte, please! | Ich möchte à la carte essen. | ɪç ˌmœçtə ɑlaˈkaʀt ˌɛsən

I just want a snack. | Ich möchte nur eine Kleinigkeit essen. | ɪç ˌmœçtə nuːʀ ˌaɪnə ˈklaɪnɪçkaɪt ˌɛsən

I would like a *generous (small)* portion, please. | Ich möchte eine *große (kleine)* Portion. | ɪç ˌmœçtə ˌaɪnə ˈɡʀoːsə (ˈklaɪnə) pɔʀˈtioːn

I must observe a strict diet. | Ich muß Diät essen. | ɪç mʊs diˌɛːt ˌɛsən

I have stomach trouble. | Ich bin magenleidend. | ɪç bɪn ˈmaːɡənˌlaɪdənt

I don't eat meat. | Ich esse kein Fleisch. | ɪç ˌɛsə kaɪn flaɪʃ

This is too heavy for me. | Das ist mir zu schwer. | das ɪst miːʀ tsu ʃveːʀ

I should like a quick meal. | Ich möchte etwas, was sehr schnell geht. | ɪç ˌmœçtə ˌɛtvas vas zeːʀ ʃnɛl ɡeːt

Will it take much time? | Wird es lange dauern? | vɪʀt ɛs ˈlaŋə ˌdauʌn

Which wine do you recommend? | Welchen Wein können Sie empfehlen? | ˌvɛlçən vaɪn ˌkœnən ziː ɛmˈpfeːlən

Do you serve wine by the glass? | Haben Sie offenen Wein? | ˌhaːbən ziː ˈɔfənən vaɪn

One *large (small)* glass, please! | Ein *großes (kleines)* Glas, bitte! | aɪn ˈɡʀoːsəs (ˈklaɪnəs) ɡlaːs ˌbɪtə

I want it *well done (underdone, medium)*. | *Gut (schwach, mittel)* gebraten, bitte. | ɡuːt (ʃvax, ˈmɪtəl) ɡəˌbʀaːtən ˌbɪtə

Would you kindly take this back? | Nehmen Sie das bitte zurück. | ˌneːmən ziː das ˌbɪtə tsuˈʀʏk

Sorry, I didn't order this. | Das habe ich nicht bestellt. | das ˌhaːbə ɪç nɪçt bəˈʃtɛlt

I wish to make a complaint. | Ich möchte mich beschweren. | ɪç ˌmœçtə mɪç bəˈʃveːʀən

The bill, please! | Die Rechnung bitte! | diː ˈʀɛçnʊŋ ˌbɪtə

Does it include service? | Ist die Bedienung einbegriffen? | ɪst diː bəˌdiːnʊŋ ˈaɪnbəˌɡʀɪfən

Sorry, you must be mistaken. | Sie müssen sich geirrt haben. | ziː ˌmʏsən zɪç ɡəˈɪʀt ˌhaːbən

This is for you. | Das ist für Sie. | das ɪst fyːʀ ziː

ash tray	der Aschbecher (-s; -)	'aʃbɛçɐ
bottle	die Flasche (-; -n)	'flaʃə
bread	das Brot (-es; -e)	bʀoːt
breakfast	das Frühstück (-s; -e)	'fʀyːʃtʏk
brown bread	das Schwarzbrot (-es; -e)	'ʃvaʀtsbʀoːt
butter	die Butter (-; 0)	'butɐ
café	das Café (-s; -s)	ka'feː
cake	der Kuchen (-s; -)	'kuːxən
cakes	das Gebäck (-s; 0)	gə'bɛk
coffee	der Kaffee (-s; 0)	'kafeː
confectionery	die Konditorei (-; -en)	kɔndito'ʀaɪ
cream	die Sahne (-; 0)	'zɑːnə
cup of tea	eine Tasse Tee	ˌaɪnə 'tasə teː
dinner	das Mittagessen / das (große) Abendessen (-s; -)	'mɪtɑːk⁷ɛsən / das ('gʀoːsə) 'ɑːbənt⁷ɛsən
eggs	Eier pl.	'aɪɐ
evening meal	das Abendessen (-s; -)	'ɑːbənt⁷ɛsən
fork	die Gabel (-; -n)	'gɑːbəl
glass	das Glas (-es; ⁻er)	glɑːs
grease	das Fett (-s; -e)	fɛt
ham	der Schinken (-s; -)	'ʃɪŋkən
honey	der Honig (-s; 0)	'hoːnɪç
jam	die Marmelade (-; -n)	maʀmə'lɑːdə
jelly	das Gelee (-s; -s)	ʒe'leː
knife	das Messer (-s; -)	'mɛsɐ
lard	das Schmalz (-es; 0)	ʃmalts
lunch	das Mittagessen (-s; -)	'mɪtɑːk⁷ɛsən
milk bar	die Milchbar (-; -s)	'mɪlçbɑːʀ
mustard	der Senf (-s; -e)	zɛnf
napkin	die Serviette (-; -n)	zɛʀ'vɪɛtə
oil	das Speiseöl (-s; -e)	'ʃpaɪzə⁷øːl
pepper	der Pfeffer (-s; -)	'pfɛfɐ
plate	der Teller (-s; -)	'tɛlɐ
portion	die Portion (-; -en)	pɔʀ'tio:n
roll	das Brötchen (-s; -)	'bʀøːtçən
salt	das Salz (-es; -e)	zalts
sausage	die Wurst (-; ⁻e)	vuʀst
set meal	das Gedeck (-s; -e)	gə'dɛk
slice of bread	eine Scheibe (Brot)	ˌaɪnə 'ʃaɪbə (bʀoːt)
small pot	das Kännchen (-s; -)	'kɛnçən
spoon	der Löffel (-s; -)	'lœfəl
sugar	der Zucker (-s; 0)	'tsukɐ
tart	die Torte (-; -n)	'tɔʀtə
tea-room	das Café (-s; -s)	ka'feː
toast	der Toast (-s; -s)	toːst
vegetarian	vegetarisch	vegə'tɑːʀɪʃ
vinegar	der Essig (-s; 0)	'ɛsɪç
waiter	der Kellner / der Ober (-s; -)	'kɛlnɐ / 'oːbɐ
waitress	die Kellnerin (-; -nen)	'kɛlnəʀɪn
whipped cream	die Schlagsahne (-; 0)	'ʃlɑːkzɑːnə
white bread	das Weißbrot (-es; -e)	'vaɪsbʀoːt
wine-list	die Weinkarte (-; -n)	'vaɪnkaʀtə

CAFÉ	tea-room	SCHNELLIMBISS
FEINKOST	delicatessen	snacks
KONDITOREI	confectionery	
LEBENSMITTEL		SELBSTBEDIENUNG
	provisions	self-service

Food and Drink (I):

Hors-d'œuvres and Principal Dishes

Entrees, Hors-d'œuvres	Vorspeisen	'fɔːʁʃpaɪzən
anchovies	Sardellen pl.	zaʁ'dɛlən
caviar	der Kaviar (-s; 0)	'kɑːvĭaːʁ
chicken salad	der Geflügelsalat (-s; -e)	gə'flyːgəlzɑˌlɑːt
cold meat	kaltes Fleisch	'kaltəs flaɪʃ
edible snails	die Weinbergschnecke (-; -n)	'vaɪnbɛʁkʃnɛkə
oysters	Austern pl.	'aʊstɐn
pâté de fois gras	die Gänseleberpastete (-; -n)	'gɛnzəleːbaˌpaˌsteːtə
puff-paste pastry	die Blätterteigpastete (-; -n)	'blɛtɐˌtaɪgpaˌsteːtə
Russian eggs	Russische Eier pl.	'ʁʊsɪʃə 'aɪɐ
sardines	Sardinen pl.	zaʁ'diːnən
Soups	**Suppen**	'zʊpən
asparagus soup	die Spargelsuppe (-; -n)	'ʃpaʁgəlzʊpə
bean soup	– Bohnensuppe	'boːnənzʊpə
beef tea	die Kraftbrühe (-; -n).	'kʁaftbʁyːə
cauliflower soup	– Blumenkohlsuppe	'bluːmənkoːlzʊpə
chicken broth	– Hühnerbrühe	'hyːnaˌbʁyːə
crayfish soup	– Krebssuppe	'kʁeːpszʊpə
fish soup	– Fischsuppe	'fɪʃzʊpə
lentil soup	– Linsensuppe	'lɪnzənzʊpə
mushroom soup	– Pilzsuppe	'pɪltszʊpə
noodle soup	– Nudelsuppe	'nuːdəlzʊpə
onion soup	– Zwiebelsuppe	'tsviːbəlzʊpə
ox-tail soup	– Ochsenschwanzsuppe	'ɔksənʃvantszʊpə
pea soup	– Erbsensuppe	'ɛʁpsənzʊpə
potato soup	– Kartoffelsuppe	kaʁ'tɔfəlzʊpə
rice soup	– Reissuppe	'ʁaɪszʊpə
tomato soup	– Tomatensuppe	to'mɑːtənzʊpə
turtle soup	– Schildkrötensuppe	'ʃɪltkʁøːtənzʊpə
vegetable soup	– Gemüsesuppe	gə'myːzəzʊpə
Fish	**Fische**	'fɪʃə
carp	der Karpfen (-s; -)	'kaʁpfən
eel	der Aal (-s; -e)	aːl
haddock	der Schellfisch (-s; -e).	'ʃɛlfɪʃ
herring	der Hering (-s; -e)	'heːʁɪŋ
mackerel	die Makrele (-; -n)	ma'kʁeːlə
perch	der Barsch (-es; -e)	baʁʃ
pike	der Hecht (-es; -e)	hɛçt
plaice	die Scholle (-; -n)	'ʃɔlə
salmon	der Lachs (-es; -e)	laks
sole	die Seezunge (-; -n)	'zeːtsʊŋə
tench	der Schlei (-s; -e)	ʃlaɪ
trout	die Forelle (-; -n)	fo'ʁɛlə
tunny	der Thunfisch (-es; -e)	'tuːnfɪʃ
turbot	der Steinbutt (-s; -s)	'ʃtaɪnbʊt
Shellfish	**Schalentiere**	'ʃɑːləntiːʁə
crab	die Krabbe (-; -n)	'kʁabə
crayfish	der Krebs (-es; -e)	kʁeːps
lobster	der Hummer (-s; -)	'hʊmɐ
shrimp	die Garnele (-; -n)	gaʁ'neːlə

18

Meat	*Fleisch*	flaɪʃ
beef	Rind	ʀɪnt
lamb	Lamm	lam
mutton	Hammel	'haməl
ox	Ochse	'ɔksə
pork	Schwein	ʃvaɪn
veal	Kalb	kalp
chop	das Kotelett *(-s; -s)*	kɔt'lɛt
fillet	das Filet *(-s; -s)*	fi'leː
fricassee	das Frikassee *(-s; 0)*	fʀikaˈseː
goulash	das Gulasch *(-es; 0)*	'guːlaʃ
grill	der Rostbraten *(-s; -)*	'ʀɔstbʀɑːtən
ragout	das Ragout *(-s; 0)*	ʀɑ'guː
roast	der Braten *(-s; -)*	'bʀɑːtən
rolled meat	die Roulade *(-; -n)*	ʀuˈlɑːdə
shnitsel	das Schnitzel *(-s; -)*	'ʃnɪtsəl
steak	das Steak *(-s; -s)*	steːk
stew	der Schmorbraten *(-s; -)*	'ʃmoːʀbʀɑːtən
brain	das Hirn *(-s; 0)*	hɪʀn
kidneys	Nieren *pl.*	'niːʀən
lights	die Lunge *(-; 0)*	'luŋə
liver	die Leber *(-; -n)*	'leːba̯
tongue	die Zunge *(-; -n)*	'tsuŋə
beefsteak	das Beefsteak *(-s; -s)*	'biːfsteːk
fillet steak	das Filetsteak *(-s; -s)*	fi'leːsteːk
roastbeef	das Roastbeef *(-s; -s)*	'ʀoːstbiːf
rumpsteak	das Rumpsteak *(-s; -s)*	'ʀumpsteːk
veal cutlet	das Kalbskotelett *(-s; -s)*	'kalpskɔt,lɛt
baby sausages	Wiener Würstchen *pl.*	'viːna̯ 'vʏʀstçən
frankfurters	Frankfurter *pl.*	'fʀaŋkfuʀta̯
frying sausages	Bratwürste *pl.*	'bʀɑːtvʏʀstə
hamburgers	Deutsches Beefsteak	'dɔʏtʃəs 'biːfsteːk
meat balls	Frika(n)dellen *pl.*	fʀika(n)'dɛlən

Game and Fowl	*Wild und Geflügel*	vɪlt ʊnt gəˈflyːgəl
hare	Hase	'hɑːzə
venison	Rotwild	'ʀoːtvɪlt
wild boar	Wildschwein	'vɪltʃvaɪn
duck	Ente	'ɛntə
goose	Gans	gans
turkey	Truthahn / Pute	'tʀuːthɑːn / 'puːtə
chicken	Huhn	huːn
cockerel	Hähnchen	'hɛːnçən
breast	Brust	bʀust
chine	Rücken	'ʀʏkən
fricassee	Frikassee	fʀika'seː
hash	Haschee	ha'ʃeː
joint	Hauptstück	'haʊptʃtʏk
leg	Keule	'kɔʏlə
ragout	Ragout	ʀɑ'guː
saddle	Kamm	kam
stew	Schmorstück	'ʃmoːʀʃtʏk

Egg Dishes	*Eierspeisen*	'aɪa̯ʃpaɪzən
boiled eggs	gekochte Eier *pl.*	gə'kɔxtə 'aɪa̯
fried eggs	Spiegeleier *pl.*	'ʃpiːgəlʔaɪa̯
omelette	das Omelett *(-s; -s)*	ɔmˈlɛt
pancake	der Pfannkuchen *(-s; -)*	'pfankuːxən
scrambled eggs	Rührei *pl.*	'ʀyːʀʔaɪa̯

19

Food and Drink (II):

Trimmings, Sweets and Beverages

Potatoes	Kartoffeln	kaʁ'tɔfəln
fried potatoes	Bratkartoffeln pl.	'bʁɑːtkaʁ₊tɔfəln
mashed potatoes	der Kartoffelbrei (-s; 0)	kaʁ'tɔfəlbʁaɪ
pommes frites.........	Pommes frites pl.	pɔm'fʁit
potato dumpling	der Kartoffelkloß (-es; ≈e)	kaʁ'tɔfəlkloːs
(boiled) potatoes	Salzkartoffeln pl.......	'zaltskaʁ₊tɔfəln
potatoes with parsley ..	Petersilienkartoffeln pl.	peːtɑ₊'ziːliənkaʁ₊tɔfəln
roast potatoes	Röstkartoffeln pl.	'ʁœstkaʁ₊tɔfəln

Processed Foods	Nährmittel	'nɛːʁmɪtəl
macaroni.............	Makkaroni pl.........	makaˈʁoːni
ravioli	Ravioli pl.	ʁɑ'vĭoːli
ribbon-macaroni......	Bandnudeln pl.	'bantnuːdəln
rice	der Reis (-; 0)	ʁaɪs
spaghetti	Spaghetti pl.	ʃpɑ'gɛti

Vegetables	Gemüse	ɡə'myːzə
artichokes	Artischocken pl.	aʁti'ʃɔkən
asparagus	der Spargel (-s; -)	'ʃpaʁɡəl
beans	Bohnen pl.	'boːnən
Brussels sprouts	der Rosenkohl (-s; 0).	'ʁoːzənkoːl
cabbage.............	der Kohl (-s; 0)......	koːl
carrots	Karotten / Möhren pl. .	ka'ʁɔtən / 'møːʁən
cauliflower	der Blumenkohl (-s; 0)	'bluːmənkoːl
chanterelles	Pfifferlinge pl.	'pfɪfɑ₊lɪŋə
chicory	die Chicorée (-; -) ...	ʃiːko'ʁeː
cucumber	die Gurke (-; -n).....	'ɡuʁkə
French beans	Grüne Bohnen pl.	'ɡʁyːnə 'boːnən
haricot beans	Weiße Bohnen pl......	'vaɪsə 'boːnən
kohlrabi	der Kohlrabi (-s; -s)..	koːl'ʁɑːbi
leek	der Porree (-s; 0).....	'pɔʁeː
mushrooms	Pilze pl.	'pɪltsə
onion	die Zwiebel (-; -n)....	'tsviːbəl
peas	Erbsen pl.	'ɛʁpsən
peppers	Paprikaschoten pl.	'papʁikaʃoːtən
pickled cabbage / sauerkraut	das Sauerkraut (-s; 0).	'zaʊə₊kʁaʊt
red cabbage	der Rotkohl (-s; 0)...	'ʁoːtkoːl
spinach	der Spinat (-s; 0).....	ʃpi'naːt
savoy	der Wirsing(kohl) (-s; 0)...........	'vɪʁzɪŋ(koːl)
tomato	die Tomate (-; -n)....	to'maːtə
white cabbage	der Weißkohl (-s; 0)..	'vaɪskoːl

Salads	Salate	za'laːtə
bean salad	der Bohnensalat (-s;-e)	'boːnənza₊laːt
celery salad	– Selleriesalat	'zɛləʁiza₊laːt
cucumber salad	– Gurkensalat	'ɡuʁkənza₊laːt
egg salad	– Eiersalat	'aɪa₊za₊laːt
endive salad	– Endiviensalat	ɛn'diːvĭənza₊laːt
green salad	der Kopfsalat (-es; -e)	'kɔpfza₊laːt
Italian salad	Italienischer Salat	ita'lĭeːnɪʃɑ₊ za'laːt
mixed salad	Gemischter Salat	ɡə'mɪʃtɑ₊ za'laːt
potato salad	der Kartoffelsalat (-s; 0)...........	kaʁ'tɔfəlza₊laːt
tomato salad	– Tomatensalat	to'maːtənza₊laːt

20

Desserts / Sweets — Nachspeisen — 'nɑːxʃpaɪzən

apple-sauce	das Apfelmus (-; 0)	'apfəlmuːs
cheese	der Käse (-s; -)	'kɛːzə
compote	das Kompott (-s; -s)	kəm'pɔt
cream	die Creme (-; -s)	kRɛːm
fruit salad	der Obstsalat (-s; -e)	'oːpstzɑˌlɑːt
ice-cream	das Speiseeis (-es; 0)	'ʃpaɪzəʔaɪs
omelet with preserves	Omelette confiture	ɔm'let kɔŋfi'tyːʁ
pudding	der Pudding (-s; -s)	'pʊdɪŋ
whipped cream	die Schlagsahne (-; 0)	'ʃlɑːkzɑːnə

Fruits — Obst — oːpst

apple	der Apfel (-s; ≃)	'apfəl
apricot	die Aprikose (-; -n)	apRi'koːzə
banana	die Banane (-; -n)	bɑ'nɑːnə
cherries	Kirschen pl.	'kɪʁʃən
cranberries	Preiselbeeren pl.	'pRaɪzəlbeːRən
dates	Datteln pl.	'datəln
figs	Feigen pl.	'faɪgən
grapefruit	die Grapefruit (-; -s)	'gRɛːpfRuːt
grapes	Weintrauben pl.	'vaɪntRaʊbən
hazel-nuts	Haselnüsse pl.	'haːzəlnysə
orange	die Apfelsine (-; -n)	apfəl'ziːnə
peach	der Pfirsich (-s; -e)	'pfɪʁzɪç
pear	die Birne (-; -n)	'bɪʁnə
pineapple	die Ananas (-; -)	'ananas
plums	Pflaumen pl.	'pflaʊmən
raspberries	Himbeeren pl.	'hɪmbeːRən
red currants	Rote Johannisbeeren pl.	'Roːtə jo'hanɪsbeːRən
strawberries	Erdbeeren pl.	'eːʁtbeːRən
tangerines	Mandarinen pl.	manda'Riːnən
walnuts	Walnüsse pl.	'valnysə

Alcoholic Drinks — Alkoholische Getränke — alko'hoːlɪʃə gə'tRɛŋkə

brandy	der Weinbrand (-s; ≃e)	'vaɪnbRant
cider	der Apfelwein (-s; 0)	'apfəlvaɪn
claret	der Rotwein (-s; -e)	'Roːtvaɪn
cognac	der Kognak (-s; -s)	'kɔnjak
liqueurs	Liköre pl.	li'køːRə
red wine	der Rotwein (-s; -e)	'Roːtvaɪn
sparkling wine	der Schaumwein (-s; -e)	'ʃaʊmvaɪn
stout	Dunkles Bier	'dʊŋkləs biːʁ

Beverages — Alkoholfreie Getränke — 'alkohoːlˌfRaɪə [gə'tRɛŋkə

apple juice	der Apfelsaft (-s; 0)	'apfəlzaft
chocolate	die Schokolade (-; 0)	ʃoko'lɑːdə
cocoa	der Kakao (-s; 0)	ka'kaʊ
coffee	der Kaffee (-s; 0)	'kafeː
fruit-juice	der Fruchtsaft (-es; ≃e)	'fRʊxtzaft
grape juice	der Traubensaft (-es; 0)	'tRaʊbənzaft
lemonade	die Limonade (-; -n)	limo'nɑːdə
milk	die Milch (-; 0)	mɪlç
milkshake	das Milchmischgetränk (-s; -e)	'mɪlçˌmɪʃɡəˌtRɛŋk
mineral water	das Mineralwasser	minə'Rɑːlvasɐ
Mocha coffee	der Mokka (-s; -s)	'məka
orangeade	die Orangeade (-; 0)	oRan'ʒɑːdə
soda	Selters	'zɛltɐs
tea	der Tee (-s; -s)	teː
tomato juice	der Tomatensaft (-es; 0)	to'mɑːtənzaft
water	das Wasser (-s; 0)	'vasɐ

Care of Person and Clothes

Hair-cut, please!	Haarschneiden bitte!	'haːʁʃnaɪdən ˌbɪtə
Just trim the hair around the neck.	Fassonschnitt bitte!	faˈsɔŋʃnɪt ˌbɪtə
Shampoo, please!	Haarwaschen bitte!	'haːʁvaʃən ˌbɪtə
Don't *cut it too short (leave it too long)*.	Nicht zu *kurz (lang)*.	nɪçt tsu kuʁts (laŋ)
I would like my hair *cold (warm)* permed.	Ich möchte eine *kalte (warme)* Dauerwelle.	ɪç ˌmœçtə ˌaɪnə 'kaltə ('vaʁmə) 'dauˌvɛlə
A water-wave, please!	Eine Wasserwelle bitte.	ˌaɪnə 'vasaˌvɛlə ˌbɪtə
A massage of the *head (face)*, please!	Eine *Kopfmassage (Gesichtsmassage)* bitte!	ˌaɪnə 'kɔpfmaˌsaːʒə (gəˈzɪçtsmaˌsaːʒə) ˌbɪtə
A *manicure (pedicure)*, please!	*Maniküre (Pediküre)* bitte!	maniˈkyːʁə (pediˈkyːʁə) ˌbɪtə
A shave, please!	Rasieren bitte!	ʁɑˈziːʁən ˌbɪtə
Dye (tinge) my hair, please!	Die Haare *färben (tönen)* bitte!	diː 'haːʁə 'fɛʁbən ('tøːnən) ˌbɪtə
How long will I have to wait?	Wie lange muß ich warten?	viː ˌlaŋə mus ɪç 'vaʁtən

---

I would like this to be dry-cleaned (dyed).	Dies muß *gereinigt (gefärbt)* werden.	diːs mus gəˈʁaɪnɪçt (gəˈfɛʁpt) ˌveːʁdən
I would like this repaired.	Ich möchte dies repariert haben.	ɪç ˌmœçtə diːs ʁepɑˈʁiːʁt ˌhaːbən
These things must be washed.	Diese Sachen müssen gewaschen werden.	ˌdiːzə 'zaxən ˌmysən gəˈvaʃən ˌveːʁdən
Please *wash carefully (use lukewarm water)*!	Bitte *vorsichtig (nur lauwarm)* waschen!	ˌbɪtə 'foːʁzɪçtɪç (nuːʁ 'lauvaʁm) 'vaʃən
would you kindly	Würden Sie mir bitte	ˌvyʁdən ziː miːʁ ˌbɪtə
– brush this suit.	– diesen Anzug ausbürsten.	– ˌdiːzən 'antsuːk 'ausbyʁstən
– press this blouse.	– diese Bluse bügeln.	– ˌdiːzə 'bluːzə 'byːgəln
– wash this dress.	– dieses Kleid waschen.	– ˌdiːzəs klaɪt 'vaʃən
– sew on this button.	– diesen Knopf annähen.	– ˌdiːzən knɔpf 'annɛːən
– repair these ladders.	– diese Maschen aufnehmen.	– ˌdiːzə 'maʃən 'aufneːmən
– wash these things.	– diese Sachen waschen.	– ˌdiːzə 'zaxən 'vaʃən
– sole these shoes.	– diese Schuhe besohlen.	– ˌdiːzə 'ʃuːə bəˈzoːlən
– re-heel these shoes.	– an diese Schuhe neue Absätze machen.	– an ˌdiːzə 'ʃuːə 'nɔʏə 'apzɛtsə ˌmaxən
– darn these socks.	– diese Strümpfe stopfen.	– ˌdiːzə 'ʃtʁʏmpfə 'ʃtɔpfən
Please don't starch *the collar (the cuffs)*!	Bitte *den Kragen (die Manschetten)* nicht stärken!	ˌbɪtə deːn 'kʁaːgən (diː man'ʃetən) nɪçt 'ʃtɛʁkən

---

BADEANSTALT	public-baths
DROGERIE	chemist's
FRISEUR	hairdresser
SCHNEIDEREI	tailor's
SCHNELLREINIGUNG	express cleaners
SCHUHMACHER	shoemaker
SEIFEN	scent-shop
WÄSCHEREI	laundry

after-shave lotion	das Rasierwasser *(-s; -)*	ʀɑ'ziːʀvasə
bath-salts	das Badesalz *(-es; -e)* .	'bɑːdəzalts
brush...............	die Bürste *(-; -n)*	'byʀstə
cake of soap	(ein) Stück Seife	(ain) ʃtyk 'zaifə
comb	der Kamm *(-es; ᵘe)*...	kam
curls	Locken *pl.*	'lɔkən
darning-cotton	das Stopfgarn *(-s; -e)* .	'ʃtɔpfgaʀn
darning-needle	die Stopfnadel *(-; -n)*.	'ʃtɔpfnɑːdəl
eau-de-Cologne	Kölnischwasser	ˌkœlniʃ'vasə
elastic band	das Gummiband *(-es; ᵘer)*	'gumibant
eyebrow pencil	der Augenbrauenstift *(-s; -e)*	'augənbʀauənʃtift
face cloth	der Waschlappen *(-s;-)*	'vaʃlapən
hairdo	die Frisur *(-; -en)*....	fʀi'zuːʀ
hairpins	Haarnadeln *pl.*	'hɑːʀnɑːdəln
lip-stick.............	der Lippenstift *(-s; -e)*	'lipənʃtift
make-up	die Schminke *(-; -n)*..	'ʃminkə
mouth-wash	das Mundwasser *(-s; -)*	'muntvasə
nail enamel	der Nagellack *(-s; -e)*.	'nɑːgəllak
nail enamel remover ...	der Nagellackentferner *(-s; -)*	'nɑːgəllakʔɛntˌfeʀnə
nail-file	die Nagelfeile *(-; -n)*..	'nɑːgəlfailə
nail-scissors	die Nagelschere *(-; -n)*	'nɑːgəlʃeːʀə
needle	die Nähnadel *(-; -n)*..	'neːnɑːdəl
pair of scissors	die Schere *(-; -n)*.....	'ʃeːʀə
pair of sun-glasses	die Sonnenbrille *(-; -n)*	'zɔnənbʀilə
patent fastener	der Druckknopf *(-es; ᵘe)*	'dʀukknɔpf
perfume.............	das Parfüm *(-s; -s)* ...	paʀ'fyːm
perm	die Dauerwelle *(-; -n)*	'dauəˌvɛlə
pins	Stecknadeln *pl.*	'ʃtɛknɑːdəln
pocket comb	der Taschenkamm *(-s; ᵘe)*	'taʃənkam
pocket-mirror	der Taschenspiegel *(-s; -)*	'taʃənʃpiːgəl
powder	der Puder *(-s; -)*......	'puːdə
razor-blades	Rasierklingen *pl.*	ʀɑ'ziːʀkliŋən
safety-pins	Sicherheitsnadeln *pl.* ..	'ziçəˌhaitsnɑːdəln
safety-razor	der Rasierapparat *(-s; -e)*	ʀɑ'ziːʀʔapaˌʀɑːt
sewing-cotton	das Nähgarn *(-s; -e)*..	'nɛːgaʀn
shampoo	das Haarwaschmittel *(-s; -)*	'hɑːʀvaʃmitəl
shaving brush	der Rasierpinsel *(-s; -)*	ʀɑ'ziːʀpinzəl
shaving-cream	die Rasiercreme *(-; -s)*	ʀɑ'ziːʀkʀɛːm
shoe-brush	die Schuhbürste *(-; -n)*	'ʃuːbyʀstə
shoe-lace	der Schnürsenkel *(-s;-)*	'ʃnyːʀzɛŋkəl
shoe-polish	die Schuhcreme *(-; -s)*	'ʃuːkʀɛːm
shower-bath	das Brausebad *(-es; ᵘer)*	'bʀauzəbɑːt
skin cream	die Hautcreme *(-; -s)*.	'hautkʀɛːm
sun-tan lotion	das Sonnen(brand)öl *(-s; 0)*	'zɔnən(bʀant)øːl
talcum powder	der Körperpuder *(-s; -)*	'kœʀpaˌpuːdə
toilet-paper	das Toilettenpapier *(-s; 0)*	tŏa'lɛtənpaˌpiːʀ
tooth-brush	die Zahnbürste *(-; -n)*	'tsɑːnbyʀstə
tooth-paste	die Zahnpasta *(-; -pasten)*	'tsɑːnpasta
zip-fastener..........	der Reißverschluß *(-sses; ᵘsse)*	'ʀaisfeʀˌʃlus

Shopping

Where can I buy ...?	Wo kann ich ... kaufen?	vo: kan ıç ... ˌkaʊfən
Is there a shop which specialises in ...?	Gibt es ein Spezialgeschäft für ...?	giːpt ɛs aın ʃpeːˈtsiɑːlɡə ˌʃɛft fyːʁ ...
Please show me something else!	Zeigen Sie mir bitte etwas anderes!	ˌtsaıɡən ziː miːʁ ˌbıtə ˌɛtvas ˈandəʁəs
I don't like the *form (colour)*.	Die *Form (Farbe)* gefällt mir nicht.	diː fɔʁm (ˈfɑːʁbə) ɡəˈfɛlt miːʁ nıçt
I think the pattern is too loud *(showy)*.	Das *Muster* ist mir zu *unruhig (auffällig)*.	das ˌmʊstɐ ıst miːʁ tsu ˈʊnruːıç (ˈaʊffɛlıç)
It should go with this.	Es muß hierzu passen.	ɛs mʊs ˈhiːʁtsu ˈpasən
I should like to try *it (the ...)* on.	Ich möchte *es (den, die, das ...)* anprobieren.	ıç ˌmœçtə ɛs (deːn, diː, das ...) ˈanpʁoːˌbiːʁən
Can I have the goods delivered?	Können Sie mir die Ware zuschicken?	ˌkœnən ziː miːʁ diː ˈvaːʁə ˈtsuːʃıkən
Please *wrap it up carefully (do it up as a present)*!	Packen Sie es bitte *gut (nett)* ein!	ˌpakən ziː ɛs ˌbıtə ɡuːt (nɛt) aın
May I have a receipt, please?	Kann ich eine Quittung haben, bitte?	kan ıç ˌaınə ˈkvıtʊŋ ˌhaːbən ˌbıtə
Please have this film developed!	Bitte entwickeln Sie diesen Film!	ˌbıtə ɛntˈvıkəln ziː ˌdiːzən fılm
I should like *one print each (one enlargement each ... by ...)*.	Ich möchte *je einen Abzug (je eine Vergrößerung ... mal ...)*.	ıç ˌmœçtə jeː ˈaınən ˈaptsuːk (jeː ˈaınə fɛʁ ˈɡʁøːsəʁʊŋ ... maːl ...)

Weights and Measures	*Maße und Gewichte*	ˈmaːsə ʊnt ɡəˈvıçtə
100 gramme (about 4 ozs)	hundert Gramm	ˈhʊndɐt ɡʁam
a quarter of a pound	ein Viertelpfund	aın ˌfıʁtəlˈpfʊnt
a pound *(half a pound)*	ein *(halbes)* Pfund	aın (ˈhalbəs) pfʊnt
one kilogramme *(half a kilogramme)*	ein *(halbes)* Kilo	aın (ˈhalbəs) ˈkiːlo
half a pint	ein Viertelliter	aın ˌfıʁtəlˈliːtɐ
two pints *(one pint)*	ein *(halber)* Liter	aın (ˈhalbɐ) ˈliːtɐ
thirty centimetres	dreißig Zentimeter	ˈdʁaısıç ˈtsɛntiˌmeːtɐ
a yard *(half a yard)*	ein *(halber)* Meter	aın (ˈhalbɐ) ˈmeːtɐ
a *(small)* parcel	ein Paket *(ein Päckchen)*	aın pɑˈkeːt (aın ˈpɛkçən)
tin / roll	die Dose / die Rolle	diː ˈdoːzə / diː ˈʁɔlə
(small) bottle	*(kleine)* Flasche	(ˈklaınə) ˈflaʃə
tube / paper bag	die Tube / die Tüte	diː ˈtuːbə / diː ˈtyːtə
some / a, one piece	einige / ein Stück	ˈaınıɡə / aın ʃtʏk
a pair / a dozen	ein Paar / ein Dutzend	aın pɑːʁ / aın ˈdʊtsənt

SHOP

ANDENKEN	souvenirs	OBST UND GEMÜSE	fruits and vegetables
AUSVERKAUF	sale		
BLUMEN	florist	OPTIKER	optician
BUCHHANDLUNG	book-shop	PAPIERWAREN	stationery
LEBENSMITTEL	grocer	SCHUHE	shoe-shop
		SÜSSWAREN	confectionery
LEDERWAREN	leather goods	TABAK	tobacconist
METZGEREI	butcher	TEXTILIEN	textiles

ball pen	der Kugelschreiber (-s; -)	'kuːgəlʃʀaɪbə
bathing costume	der Badeanzug (-s; ⁺e)	'baːdəʔantsuːk
bathing trunks	die Badehose (-; -n)	'baːdəhoːzə
bath-robe	der Bademantel (-s; ⁺)	'baːdəmantəl
belt	der Gürtel (-s; -)	'gʏʀtəl
blouse	die Bluse (-; -n)	'bluːzə
brassière	der Büstenhalter (-s; -)	'bʏstənhaltə
button	der Knopf (-es; ⁺e)	knɔpf
cap	die Mütze (-; -n)	'mʏtsə
cardigan	die Strickjacke (-; -n)	'ʃtʀɪkjakə
cigarettes	Zigaretten pl.	tsigaˈʀɛtən
cigars	Zigarren pl.	tsiˈgaʀən
collar	der Kragen (-s; -)	'kʀaːgən
colour film	der Farbfilm (-s; -e)	'faʀpfɪlm
diary	das Notizbuch (-es; ⁺er)	noˈtiːtsbuːx
dress	das Kleid (-es; -er)	klaɪt
envelopes	Briefumschläge pl.	'bʀiːfʔʊmʃlɛːgə
fountain-pen	der Füllhalter (-s; -)	'fʏlhaltə
gloves	Handschuhe pl.	'hantʃuːə
handkerchief	das Taschentuch (-s; ⁺er)	'taʃəntuːx
hat	der Hut (-es; ⁺e)	huːt
ink	die Tinte (-; -n)	'tɪntə
jacket	die Jacke (-; -n)	'jakə
lighter	das Feuerzeug (-s; -e)	'fɔʏɐtsɔʏk
matches	Zündhölzer pl.	'tsʏnthœltsə
neckerchief	das Halstuch (-s; ⁺er)	'halstuːx
night-gown	das Nachthemd (-s; -en)	'naxthɛmt
night-shirt	das Briefpapier (-s; 0)	'bʀiːfpaˌpiːʀ
note paper	Nylonstrümpfe pl.	'naɪlɔnʃtʀʏmpfə
nylons	der Schlüpfer (-s; -)	'ʃlʏpfə
panties	der Druckknopf (-es; ⁺e)	'dʀʊkknɔpf
patent fastener	der Bleistift (-s; -e)	'blaɪʃtɪft
pencil	der Pfeifentabak (-s; -e)	'pfaɪfəntabak
pipe-tobacco	Spielkarten pl.	'ʃpiːlkaʀtən
playing-cards	der Preis (-es; -e)	pʀaɪs
price	der Pullover (-s; -)	pʊˈloːvə
pull-over	das Portemonnaie (-s; -s)	pɔʀtmoˈneː
purse	der Schlafanzug (-s; ⁺e)	'ʃlaːfʔantsuːk
pyjamas	Sandalen pl.	zanˈdaːlən
sandals	Damenbinden pl.	'daːmənbɪndən
sanitary towels	der Schal (-s; -s)	ʃaːl
scarf	das Oberhemd (-s; -en)	'oːbɐˌhɛmt
shirt	Schuhe pl.	'ʃuːə
shoes	der Rock (-s; ⁺e)	ʀɔk
skirt	der Unterrock (-s; ⁺e)	'ʊntɐˌʀɔk
slip	Socken pl.	'zɔkən
socks	Strümpfe pl.	'ʃtʀʏmpfə
stockings	der Anzug (-s; ⁺e)	'antsuːk
suit	der Strumpfhalter (-s; -)	'ʃtʀʊmpfhaltə
suspender-belt	der Schlips (-es; -e)	ʃlɪps
tie	das Handtuch (-s; ⁺er)	'hanttuːx
towel	Hosen pl.	'hoːzən
trousers	der Regenschirm (-s; -e)	'ʀeːgənʃɪʀm
umbrella	das Unterhemd (-s; -en)	'ʊntɐˌhɛmt
vest	die Brieftasche (-; -n)	'bʀiːftaʃə
wallet		

SHOP

25

Customs, Bank, Police, and Post Office

A the Border / An der Grenze / an deːʀ 'gʀɛntsə

English	German	Phonetic
Shall I open my suitcase?	Soll ich den Koffer aufmachen?	zɔl ɪç deːn 'kɔfɐ 'aufmaxən
*Have you anything to declare, dutiable goods?	*Haben Sie etwas zu verzollen?	ˌhaːbən ziː ˌɛtvas tsu fɛʀ'tsɔlən
Only things for my personal use.	Nur persönliche Dinge.	nuːʀ pɛʀ'zøːnlɪçə 'dɪŋə
*Please open this one!	Öffnen Sie das bitte!	'œfnən ziː das ˌbɪtə
*That's allright.	In Ordnung!	ɪn 'ɔʀdnʊŋ
*This is dutiable.	Das ist zollpflichtig!	das ɪst 'tsɔlpflɪçtɪç
*You must give security for this.	Dafür müssen Sie Kaution hinterlegen.	'daːfyːʀ ˌmʏsən ziː kau'tioːn hɪntɐˌleːgən
*Have you any luggage in the luggage van?	Haben Sie Gepäck im Gepäckwagen?	ˌhaːbən ziː gə'pɛk ɪm gə'pɛkvaːgən

Money Exchange / Geldwechsel / 'gɛltvɛksəl

English	German	Phonetic
Where can I change some money?	Wo kann ich Geld wechseln?	voː kan ɪç gɛlt ˌvɛksəln
Please change this into ...?	Wechseln Sie mir dies bitte in ...	'vɛksəln ziː miːʀ diːs ˌbɪtə ɪn ...
What is the exchange rate for ...?	Wie ist der Kurs für ...?	viː ɪst deːʀ kuʀs fyːʀ ...

At the Police Station / Auf der Polizei / auf deːʀ poli'tsai

English	German	Phonetic
I want to report something.	Ich möchte eine Anzeige erstatten.	ɪç ˌmœçtə ˌainə 'antsaigə ɛʀ'ʃtatən
I have had *my* ... stolen.	Man hat mir *mein (meine, meinen)* ... gestohlen.	man hat miːʀ main (ˌmainə, ˌmainən) ... gə'ʃtoːlən
I lost *my* ...	Ich habe *meinen (meine, mein)* ... verloren.	ɪç ˌhaːbə ˌmainən (ˌmainə, main) ... fɛʀ'loːʀən
Please inform my consulate.	Verständigen Sie bitte mein Konsulat.	fɛʀ'ʃtɛndigən ziː ˌbɪtə main konzu'laːt
*Can you name witnesses?	Haben Sie Zeugen?	ˌhaːbən ziː 'tsɔygən

At the Post-Office / Auf der Post / auf deːʀ pɔst

English	German	Phonetic
What is the postage on this letter?	Wie hoch ist das Porto für diesen Brief?	viː hoːx ɪst das 'pɔʀto fyːʀ ˌdiːzən bʀiːf
I should like ...	Ich möchte ...	ɪç 'mœçtə ...
– to register this letter.	– diesen Brief eingeschrieben schicken.	– ˌdiːzən bʀiːf 'aingəˌʃʀiːbəˌ ˌʃikən
– to send a telegram (reply-paid).	– ein Telegramm (mit Rückantwort) aufgeben.	– ain tele'gʀam (mit 'ʀʏkʔantvɔʀt) ˌaufgeːbən
– to have a long-distance call put through to ... (as a personal call).	– ein Gespräch nach ... aufgeben (mit Voranmeldung).	– ain gə'ʃpʀɛːç naːx ... ˌaufgeːbən(mit 'foːʀʔanmɛldʊŋ)
I want to contact a friend by 'phone, could you assist me, please?	Ich möchte einen Freund anrufen, wollen Sie mir bitte helfen?	ɪç ˌmœçtə ˌainən fʀɔynt ˌanruːfən, ˌvɔlən ziː miːʀ ˌbɪtə 'hɛlfən
*Sorry, there is no reply.	Der Teilnehmer antwortet nicht.	deːʀ 'tailneːmɐ 'antvɔʀtət nɪçt
*Sorry, number engaged.	Die Nummer ist besetzt.	diː 'numɐ ɪst bə'zɛtst
*Sorry, we were cut off.	Die Leitung ist gestört.	diː 'laitʊŋ ɪst gə'ʃtøːʀt

address	die Adresse *(-; -n)*	a'dʀɛsə
by air mail	mit Luftpost	mɪt 'lʊftpɔst
car documents	Wagenpapiere *pl.*	'vɑːgənpɑˌpiːʀə
counter	der Schalter *(-s; -)*	'ʃaltɐ
customs	die Zollabfertigung *(-; -en)*	'tsɔlʔapfɛʀtiguŋ
directory	das Adreßbuch *(-es; ⁿer)*	a'dʀɛsbuːx
express delivery	mit Eilboten	mɪt 'aɪlboːtən
foreign exchange	Devisen *pl.*	de'viːzən
form	das Formular *(-s; -e)*	fɔʀmu'lɑːʀ
identity card	der Ausweis *(-es; -e)*	'aʊsvaɪs
letter	der Brief *(-es; -e)*	bʀiːf
letter of credit	der Kreditbrief *(-s; -e)*	kʀe'diːtbʀiːf
local call	das Ortsgespräch *(-s; -e)*	'ɔʀtsgəˌʃpʀɛːç
long-distance call	das Ferngespräch *(-s; -e)*	'fɛʀngəˌʃpʀɛːç
parcel	das Paket *(-s; -e)*	pa'keːt
passport	der Paß *(-sses; ⁿsse)*	pas
passport inspection	die Paßkontrolle *(-; -n)*	'paskɔnˌtʀɔlə
paying-in form	die Zahlkarte *(-; -n)*	'tsɑːlkaʀtə
postage	das Porto *(-s; Porti)*	'pɔʀto
postal order	die Postanweisung *(-; -en)*	'pɔstʔanvaɪzuŋ
postcard	die Postkarte *(-; -n)*	'pɔstkaʀtə
post office	das Postamt *(-s; ⁿer)*	'pɔstʔamt
rate of exchange	der Wechselkurs *(-es; -e)*	'vɛksəlkuʀs
registration *(with the police)*	*(polizeiliche)* Anmeldung	(poli'tsaɪlɪçə) 'anmɛlduŋ
remittance	die Überweisung *(-; -en)*	yːbɐ'vaɪzuŋ
scales	die Briefwaage *(-; -n)*	'bʀiːfvaːgə
sender	der Absender *(-s; -)*	'apzɛndɐ
signature	die Unterschrift *(-;-en)*	'untɐʃʀɪft
stamps	Briefmarken *pl.*	'bʀiːfmaʀkən
telegram	das Telegramm *(-s;-e)*	tele'gʀam
telegraphic	telegrafisch	tele'gʀɑːfɪʃ
telegraph form	das Telegrammformular *(-s; -e)*	tele'gʀamfɔʀmuˌlɑːʀ
telephone box	die Telefonzelle *(-; -n)*	tele'foːntsɛlə
telephone directory	das Telefonbuch *(-s; ⁿer)*	tele'foːnbuːx
telephone number	die Telefonnummer *(-; -n)*	tele'foːnumɐ
teleprint	das Fernschreiben *(-s; -)*	'fɛʀnʃʀaɪbən
traveller's cheque	der Reisescheck *(-s; -s)*	'ʀaɪzəʃɛk

FERNSPRECHER	telephone	KASSE	cash-desk
FEUERMELDER	fire-alarm	KONTROLLPUNKT	check-point
FEUERWEHR	fire-brigade	LEIHHAUS	pawnshop
FUNDBÜRO	lost-property office	POLIZEI	police
		POSTAMT	post office
GELDWECHSEL	money ex-change	POSTLAGERND	poste restante
		SPARKASSE	savings-bank
GRENZE	bɔrder	ZOLL	customs

27

First Aid

Can you recommend a good general practitioner (specialist for ...)?	Können Sie mir einen guten Arzt (Spezialisten für ...) empfehlen?	ˌkœnən ziː miːʀ ˌaɪnən ˈɡuːtən aːʀtst (ʃpeːtsɪaˈlɪsten fyːʀ ...) ɛmˈpfeːlən
Where is the nearest pharmacy (first-aid station)?	Wo ist die nächste Apotheke (Unfallstation)?	voː ɪst diː ˈnɛːçstə apoˈteːkə (ˈʊnfalˌʃtaˌtsɪoːn)
*What's the trouble?	Welche Beschwerden haben Sie?	ˌvɛlçə bəˈʃveːʀdən ˌhaːbən ziː
I have a pain here.	Ich habe hier Schmerzen.	ɪç ˌhaːbə hiːʀ ˈʃmɛʀtsən
I suffer from ...	Ich leide an ...	ɪç ˈlaɪdə an ...
When should I call again?	Wann soll ich wiederkommen?	van zɔl ɪç ˈviːdəˌkɔmən
When (how often) should I take this?	Wann (wie oft) muß ich das einnehmen?	van (viː ˈɔft) mʊs ɪç das ˈaɪnneːmən
Can this tooth be filled?	Kann der Zahn plombiert werden?	kan deːʀ tsaːn plɔmˈbiːʀt ˌveːʀdən
Is it necessary to extract this tooth?	Muß der Zahn gezogen werden?	mʊs deːʀ tsaːn ɡəˈtsoːɡən ˌveːʀdən

Diseases	*Krankheiten*	ˈkʀaŋkhaɪtən
appendicitis	die Blinddarmentzündung	ˈblɪntdaʀmˀɛnˌtsʏndʊŋ
boil	das Geschwür (-s; -e).	ɡəˈʃvyːʀ
burn................	die Verbrennung (-; -en)	fɛʀˈbʀɛnʊŋ
cold	der Schnupfen (-s; 0).	ˈʃnʊpfən
constipation	die Verstopfung (-; 0).	fɛʀˈʃtɔpfʊŋ
cough	der Husten (-s; 0)....	ˈhuːstən
diabetes.............	die Zuckerkrankheit (-; 0)	ˈtsʊkəˌkʀaŋkhaɪt
diarrhoea	der Durchfall (-s; 0)..	ˈdʊʀçfal
dislocation	die Verrenkung (-; 0).	fɛʀˈʀɛŋkʊŋ
faint	die Ohnmacht (-; -en)	ˈoːnmaxt
flu	die Grippe (-; 0).....	ˈɡʀɪpə
fracture	der (Knochen-)Bruch (-s; ⁼e)	(ˈknɔxən-)bʀʊx
grumbling appendix....	die Blinddarmreizung (-; -en)	ˈblɪntdaʀmʀaɪtsʊŋ
haemorrhage	die Blutung (-; -en)...	ˈbluːtʊŋ
headache	Kopfschmerzen pl.....	ˈkɔpfʃmɛʀtsən
heartburn	das Sodbrennen (-s; 0)	ˈzoːtbʀɛnən
influenza	die Grippe (-; 0).....	ˈɡʀɪpə
nose-bleeding	das Nasenbluten (-s; 0)	ˈnaːzənbluːtən
pain in the stomach	Magenschmerzen pl....	ˈmaːɡənʃmɛʀtsən
pneumonia	die Lungenentzündung (-; 0)	ˈlʊŋənˀɛnˌtsʏndʊŋ
poisoning	die Vergiftung (-; -en)	fɛʀˈɡɪftʊŋ
rheumatism...........	der Rheumatismus (-ses; 0)	ʀɔymaˈtɪsmʊs
sore throat	Halsschmerzen pl......	ˈhalsʃmɛʀtsən
stomach cramp........	Magenkrämpfe pl......	ˈmaːɡənkʀɛmpfə
stroke	der Schlaganfall (-s; ⁼e)	ˈʃlaːkˀanfal
sunburn..............	der Sonnenbrand(-s; 0)	ˈzɔnənbʀant
sunstroke............	der Sonnenstich (-s; 0)	ˈzɔnənʃtɪç
suppuration...........	die Vereiterung (-; 0).	fɛʀˈˀaɪtəʀʊŋ
toothache	Zahnschmerzen pl.	ˈtsaːnʃmɛʀtsən

adhesive plaster	das Heftpflaster (-s; -)	'hɛftpflastə
ambulance	der Krankenwagen (-s; -)	'kraŋkənvɑːgən
appendix	der Blinddarm (-s; 0) .	'blɪntdaʁm
bandage	die Binde (-; -n)	'bɪndə
bladder	die Blase (-; -n)	'blɑːzə
blood-pressure	der Blutdruck (-s; 0)..	'bluːtdʁʊk
bone	der Knochen (-s; -)...	'knɔxən
chemist's shop	die Apotheke (-; -n)..	apo'teːkə
crown	die (Zahn-)Krone (-; -n)	(tsɑːn-)'kʁoːnə
dressing............	der Verband (-es; ⁼e)	fɛʁ'bant
fever	das Fieber (-s; 0).....	'fiːbə
gall	die Galle (-; -n)......	'galə
heart	das Herz (-ens; -en)...	hɛʁts
hospital	das Krankenhaus (-es; ⁼er)	'kraŋkənhaʊs
inflammation	die Entzündung(-;-en)	ɛn'tsʏndʊŋ
injury	die Verletzung (-; -en)	fɛʁ'lɛtsʊŋ
intestine	der Darm (-s; ⁼e).....	daʁm
kidneys	Nieren pl.	'niːʁən
laxative	das Abführmittel (-s;-)	'apfyːʁmɪtəl
liver	die Leber (-; 0)	'leːbə
lungs	die Lunge (-; -n).....	'lʊŋə
medicine	die Arznei (-; -en)....	aːʁts'naɪ
muscles	Muskeln pl.	'mʊskəln
nerve	der Nerv (-s; -en)	nɛʁf
ointment	die Salbe (-; -n)......	'zalbə
operation	die Operation (-; -en).	opəʁa'tsioːn
pulse	der Puls (-es; -e)	pʊls
sleeping pill	das Schlafmittel (-s; -)	'ʃlɑːfmɪtəl
stomach	der Magen (-s; ⁼).....	'mɑːgən
surgical wool	die Verbandwatte(-; 0)	fɛʁ'bantvatə
thermometer	das Thermometer (-s; -)	tɛʁmo'meːtə
thyroid gland	die Schilddrüse (-; -n)	'ʃɪltdʁyːzə
tonsils	Mandeln pl...........	'mandəln
windpipe	die Luftröhre (-; -n)..	'lʊftʁøːʁə
X-ray photograph	die Röntgenaufnahme (-; -n)	'ʁœntgənaʊfnɑːmə

APOTHEKE	pharmacy	KINDERARZT	children's specialist
BEREITSCHAFTS-ARZT	doctor on call	NACHTDIENST	night-duty
CHIRURG	surgeon	NOTRUF	emergency call
ERSTE HILFE	first aid	ORTHOPÄDE	orthopaedist
FRAUENARZT	gynaecologist	SPRECHSTUNDE	consulting hour
HALS-, NASEN- UND OHRENARZT	ear, nose and throat specialist	UNFALLSTATION	first-aid station
HEBAMME	midwife	WARTEZIMMER	waitingroom
INTERNIST	internist	ZAHNARZT	dental surgeon

Recreation and Entertainment

Where can I get tickets for ...?	Wo bekommt man Karten für ...?	voː bə̩kɔmt man ˈkaʁtən fyːʁ ...
When will the advance booking start?	Wann beginnt der Vorverkauf?	van bə̩gɪnt deːʁ ˈfoːʁfɛʁ̩kauf
When will the performance commence?	Wann beginnt die Vorstellung?	van bə̩gɪnt diː ˈfoːʁʃtɛluŋ
How long will the meeting last?	Wie lange dauert die Veranstaltung?	viː ˈlaŋə ˈdauᴧt diː fɛʁ̩ˀanʃtaltuŋ
Are there any tickets left for ...?	Gibt es noch Karten für ...?	giːpt ɛs nɔx ˈkaʁtən fyːʁ ...
Have you some good seats left for ...?	Haben Sie noch gute Plätze für ...?	ˌhaːbən ziː nɔx ˈguːtə ˈplɛtsə fyːʁ ...
Which are the best seats?	Welches sind die besten Plätze?	ˈvɛlçəs zɪnt diː ˈbɛstən ˈplɛtsə
I want ... tickets for ...., please.	Geben Sie mir bitte ... Karten für ...	ˈgeːbən ziː miːʁ ̩bɪtə ... ˈkaʁtən fyːʁ ...
I should like to book ... tickets for ...	Ich möchte ... Karten für ... vorbestellen.	ɪç ̩mœçtə ... ˈkaʁtən fyːʁ ... ˈfoːʁbə̩ʃtɛlən
When must I collect the tickets?	Bis wann muß ich die Karten abholen?	bɪs van mus ɪç diː ˈkaʁtən ˈaphoːlən
Are the seats reserved?	Sind die Plätze numeriert?	zɪnt diː ̩plɛtsə numəˈʁiːʁt
I would like to *exchange (return)* these tickets.	Ich möchte diese Karten *umtauschen (zurückgeben)*.	ɪç ̩mœçtə ̩diːzə ̩kaʁtən ˈumtauʃən (tsuˈʁʏkgeːbən)
Is the film in the original?	Läuft der Film im Original?	lɔyft deːʁ fɪlm ɪm ɔʁigiˈnaːl
Has this film been dubbed?	Ist der Film synchronisiert?	ɪst deːʁ fɪlm zynkʁoniˈziːʁt
Has this film sub-titles?	Hat der Film Untertitel?	hat deːʁ fɪlm ˈuntᴧtiːtəl
*There are only tickets left *for (at)* ...	Es gibt nur noch Karten *für (zu)* ...	ɛs giːpt nuːʁ nɔx ̩kaʁtən fyːʁ (tsuː) ...
*There are no seats left.	Es ist alles ausverkauft.	ɛs ɪst ˈaləs ˈausfɛʁ̩kauft
Can I hire ...	Kann man (*hier*) ...	kan man (hiːʁ) ...
– a bathing costume?	– einen Badeanzug	– ̩ainən ˈbaːdəˀantsuːk
– bathing trunks?	– eine Badehose	– ̩ainə ˈbaːdəhoːzə
– a towel?	– ein Handtuch leihen?	– ain ˈhanttuːx ˈlaiən
Is the water very deep?	Ist es hier sehr tief?	ɪst ɛs hiːʁ zeːʁ tiːf
What is the temperature of the water?	Wie warm ist das Wasser?	viː vaʁm ɪst das ˈvasᴧ
How far may I swim out?	Wie weit darf man hinausschwimmen?	viː ˈvait daʁf man hɪˈnausʃvimən

AUSVERKAUFT			KABARETT	cabaret
	full house		KINO	cinema
BADEANSTALT			REVUE	musical
	baths		THEATER	theatre
BADEN VERBOTEN			VARIETÉ	variety theatre
	bathing prohibited			

advance booking	der Vorverkauf	'foːɐfɛɐ,kauf
bathing beach	der Badestrand *(-es; 0)*	'baːdəʃtʁant
bathing-cabin	die Umkleidekabine *(-; -n)*	'umklaɪdəka,biːnə
beach-chair	der Strandkorb *(-es; ⁼e)*	'ʃʁantkɔɐp
booking office	der Kartenverkauf *(-s; 0)*	'kaɐtənfɛɐ,kauf
box	die Loge *(-; -n)*	'loːʒə
boxing match	der Boxkampf *(-es; ⁼e)*	'bɔkskampf
box office	die Kasse *(-; -n)*	'kasə
cinema	das Kino *(-s; -s)*	'kiːnoː
circus	der Zirkus *(-ses; -se)*..	'tsɪɐkus
cloak-room..........	die Garderobe *(-; -n)*.	gaɐd(ə)'ʁoːbə
comedy	das Lustspiel *(-s; -e)*.	'lustʃpiːl
concert	das Konzert *(-s; -e)*...	kɔn'tsɛɐt
dance hall...........	die Tanzbar *(-; -s)* ...	'tantsbaːɐ
deck-chair	der Liegestuhl *(-s; ⁼e)*.	'liːgəʃtuːl
drama	das Drama *(-s; Dramen)*	'dʁaːma
dress-circle	der Rang *(-es; ⁼e)*....	ʁaŋ
educational film	der Kulturfilm *(-s; -e)*	kul'tuːɐfɪlm
football match	das Fußballspiel *(-s; -e)*	'fuːsbalʃpiːl
gambling casino	das Spielkasino *(-s; -s)*	'ʃpiːlka,ziːno
golf-links	der Golfplatz *(-es; ⁼e)*	'gɔlfplats
horse-race	das Pferderennen *(-s; -)*	'pfeːɐdəʁɛnən
life-belt	der Rettungsring *(-s; -e)*	'ʁɛtuŋsʁɪŋ
lifeguard	der Rettungsschwimmer *(-s; -)*	'ʁɛtuŋsʃvɪmɐ
musical	die Revue *(-; -n)*.....	ʁe'vyː
newsreel	die Wochenschau *(-; -en)*	'vɔxənʃau
night club	das Nachtlokal *(-s; -e)*	'naxtlo,kaːl
open-air theatre	die Freilichtbühne *(-; -n)*	'fʁaɪlɪçtbyːnə
(opera) glass	das Opernglas *(-es; ⁼er)*	'oːpɐnglaːs
opera (house)	die Oper *(-; -n)*......	'oːpɐ
paddling boat	das Paddelboot *(-s; -e)*	'padəlboːt
play	das Schauspiel *(-s; -e)*.	'ʃauʃpiːl
playbill	das Theaterprogramm *(-s; -e)*	te'aːtɐpʁoː,gʁam
programme..........	das Programm *(-s; -e)*	pʁoː'gʁam
race-course	die Rennbahn *(-; -en)*	'ʁɛnbaːn
rowing-boat	das Ruderboot *(-es; -e)*	'ʁuːdɐboːt
sailing-boat..........	das Segelboot *(-es; -e)*	'zeːgəlboːt
seat *(theatre)*	der *(Theater-)* Platz *(-es; ⁼e)*	(te'aːtɐ)plats
ski	Skier *pl.*	'ʃiːɐ
stadium.............	das Stadion *(-s; -ien)* .	'ʃtaːdɪɔn
stall	der Orchestersitz *(-es; -e)*	ɔɐ'kɛstɐzɪts
stalls	das Parkett *(-s; 0)*....	paɐ'kɛt
sunshade	der Sonnenschirm *(-s; -e)*	'zɔnənʃɪɐm
supporting programme .	das Beiprogramm *(-s; -e)*	'baɪpʁoː,gʁam
swimming-bath	das Schwimmbad *(-s; ⁼er)*	'ʃvɪmbaːt
tennis court	der Tennisplatz *(-es; ⁼e)*	'tɛnɪsplats
wrestling match	der Ringkampf *(-es; ⁼e)*	'ʁɪŋkampf
zoological gardens	der Zoo *(-s; -s)*	tsoː

Index